A WOMAN OF
ALL SEASONS

Also by Paula Harris…

Becoming Transformed

(A New Way, A New You)

A WOMAN OF ALL SEASONS

(Daily Divine Deliverance)

A New and Refreshing View!

By
Paula Harris

iUniverse, Inc.
New York   Bloomington

iUniverse books may be ordered through booksellers or by contacting:

iUniverse
1663 Liberty Drive
Bloomington, IN 47403
www.iuniverse.com
1-800-Authors (1-800-288-4677)

ISBN: 978-1-4401-2294-1 (pbk)
ISBN: 978-1-4401-2295-8 (ebk)

Library of Congress Control Number: 2009923046

Printed in the United States of America
iUniverse rev. date: 2/24/09

DEDICATION

This book is dedicated first and foremost to my Lord and Savior, Jesus Christ, for He is the One who transformed me into *A Woman of All Seasons.* Second, it is dedicated to those used by Him as *precious* refining tools in this process: William (my loving husband); Andre', Aaron and Arlen (my three sons); Heather (Arlen's wife); Caeli, Arlen, Jr. and Ayden (my grandchildren). It is a result of receiving your love and giving love in return that I am now able to savor each season of my life.

CONTENTS

Contents

ACKNOWLEDGMENTS

A heartfelt thank you to the Board of Directors (Irvin, Kae, Pat, Penny and William), Ministry Coordinators (Betty, Jane, Kathy, Louise, Patty, Pauline and Rachel), Prayer Partners and all of the supporters of Transformed Worldwide Ministries who have made it possible to get this book into the hands of women.

My abundant gratitude to Tyreta, Pat and the Women's Ministry at Montco Bible Fellowship who first asked me to speak on this topic at their retreat.

Finally, included in this bond of love is Susan, Melissa, iUniverse and all the women who helped to proof read the first draft of this book. Additionally, I dare not neglect to mention all the friends who surrounded me and spurred me on in the faith. My eternal gratitude is yours!

HOW TO USE THIS LESSON MATERIAL

Knowing you are one beloved of God, it is in faith that you can approach this material with the expectation of spiritual cleansing and refreshment through the power of His Eternal Word. It is with this in mind that the lesson material is saturated with Scripture and written in an easy format that accommodates both individual and group study.

Individual Study:

If you would like to study this material privately, may I recommend that you set aside a time and place to meet with the Lord that eliminates as much distraction as possible. Please do not be legalistic about these things, as Jesus is more concerned with your heart attitude than your performance in completing each day's assignments.

The material is written so you can complete it in one month's time (four weeks). Each of the four weekly sessions contains five daily assignments for Monday through Friday. On the weekend, review or meditate on what you have learned throughout the week.

Remember, the purpose of this book is to develop a more personal relationship with Jesus than it is to gain head knowledge or complete a goal. Therefore, go at your own pace. If you cannot complete an entire lesson in one day, that is fine. Go at a pace that allows you to digest what is being said to you personally so that you may grow stronger and not be spiritually malnourished. Thus, if it takes you several months to complete this book, it will be time well spent.

Make a commitment to complete this book. Use a notebook to jot down your thoughts if there is not enough room to do so in the book. Before you begin each lesson, prayerfully ask the Holy Spirit to teach you and increase your understanding. As you approach this time, expect God to speak to you through His Word as well as through this lesson material. Do not rush or be in a hurry. Regardless of the challenge it may present, determine right now to be obedient to His leading. It is important not to put off what He directs you to do. At the conclusion of each day's time, thank Him for what you have learned. Once you have completed the entire lesson book, continue to grow in His Word. Also, you can contact Transformed Worldwide Ministries for the four-CD set that goes along with this lesson material. There are also additional lessons on CD to help you.

<u>Group Study:</u>

If you would like to study this material in a group, it does not matter whether you do so with two or more individuals. You may want to meet in someone's home or in a public setting. I would like to recommend that you set aside a time and place to meet with the Lord that is convenient for all so attendance will not be sporadic. However, please do not be legalistic about these things, as Jesus is more concerned with everyone's heart attitude than their performance in completing each day's assignments.

The material is written so that you can complete it in one month's time (four weeks). Each of the four weekly sessions has five daily assignments for Monday through Friday. On the weekend, review or meditate on what you have learned throughout the week.

The daily assignments can be completed ahead of time before each individual meets with the rest of the group on the assigned day. Once together, each woman can share her insights and how she answered the questions presented. To keep order and not have one person dominate all the time, one person should be assigned as the group leader to keep things flowing in a timely manner. Instead of getting into elaborate decorations or food preparation, eliminate these items or keep them very simple. The focus is on Jesus and His Word.

Remember, the whole purpose of this book is to develop a more personal relationship with Jesus than it is to gain head knowledge or complete a goal. Therefore, go at your own pace. If the group needs to spread out the lesson material over several months, that is fine. The lesson material is flexible so it can be completed at a pace that is comfortable for the whole group. The pace should allow the group to digest what is being said to them personally so they may grow stronger and not be spiritually malnourished. If it takes more time to complete this book, it will be time well spent.

On the first day, read the following to those participating: Make a commitment to complete this book. Use a notebook to jot down your thoughts if there is not enough room to do so in the book. Before you begin each lesson, prayerfully ask the Holy Spirit to teach you and increase your understanding. As you approach this time, expect God to speak to you through His Word and this lesson material. Do not rush or be in a hurry. Regardless of the challenge it may present, determine right now to be obedient to His leading. It is important not to put off what He directs you to do. At the conclusion of each day's time, thank Him for what you are learning. Once you have completed the entire lesson book, continue to grow in His Word.

Also, you can contact Transformed Worldwide Ministries for the four-CD set that goes along with this lesson material. There are also additional lessons available on CD to help you.

Now let's begin this wonderful journey of becoming "A Woman of **All** Seasons!"

A WOMAN OF **ALL** SEASONS
(Daily Divine Deliverance)

INTRODUCTION:

Please ponder a few questions for a moment. Are you happy in this season of your life? Are you burnt out and left with no hope of anything ever changing for you? Are you able to enjoy what you have presently? Is there satisfaction in your accomplishments up to this point? Does your past keep you from taking a positive step toward your future? Do you feel overwhelmed by the challenges confronting you in this season of your life?

The tsunami, hurricane Katrina, California mud slides, and snow in Hawaii are recent reminders that there are times and seasons over which we have little or no control. The same is true for each season of a woman's life. She may laugh or weep, love or hate, plant or uproot during her journey. Nevertheless, she can learn to glance at her struggles, but gaze upon His sovereignty. May our time together be one of renewal, as we receive wisdom and encouragement for each season of our life.

Often when seasons are used as an analogy of a woman's life, the seasons represent the various stages of her age. "Spring" may be when a woman is still under the security of her parents' home or college days; "summer" may be the time when she has established her own home, career, and/or family; "autumn" may be a time of menopause, being a caregiver or an empty nester; and "winter" may be a time of retirement, widowhood, or of being a great grandmother.

In contrast, our study will use the analogy of seasons, but in a different way. "Spring" will represent a season of gladness; "summer" will represent a season of sadness; "autumn" will represent a season of change or transition; and "winter" will represent a season of stillness. Having taught this lesson to groups of women, they have appreciated the seasons represented in this manner, as women normally *cycle in and out* of these seasons regardless of age, marital status, careers, or lifestyles.

Looking into the perfect law of liberty (James 1:25), we will glean wisdom from Ecclesiastes, Chapter 3, to understand how to be a victorious woman in all seasons. The theme of Ecclesiastes is only in God does life have meaning and true pleasure. Without Him nothing satisfies, but with him we find satisfaction and enjoyment. True pleasure comes only when we acknowledge and revere God. Therefore, we will prayerfully seek what our Father has revealed in Ecclesiastes so that by the acknowledgement and reverence of Him, we may enjoy each season, come what may.

Come journey with me as we experience daily our Father's Divine deliverance and are transformed into a woman of all seasons.

SESSION 1
WEEK 1: Seeing Your Season

DAY 1: Similar, But Not the Same

Are you a comparison shopper? If you went shopping with me, you might become frustrated. I have no problem going from store to store comparing an item to make sure I am getting the best value and bargain for my money. My husband can go into a store to find the item he wants, and it does not matter whether another store may have it on sale or in a variety of colors, he will gladly purchase it and go home.

With the thunder of media, magazines, and society's pressures, it is easy to succumb to the storms of comparison. However, it's one thing to compare an item such as a vase, and another to compare you in any way with another woman.

I was once given a pair of jeans as a gift, but when I put them on, the waist was below my belly button. After giving birth to three healthy boys, would you believe that my abs do not resemble those of Halle Berry? Wearing these jeans was a new experience for me even though I wore a very long blouse to cover my midriff. I think the last time I wore something similar was when I was a young teen with bellbottom hip huggers covered with huge blue-and-white polka dots. Nevertheless, I found myself looking around to see how other women my age were dealing with this fashion. Finally, by the end of the day it did not matter if every woman in my church or Pennsylvania wore this style; I decided to do what was best for me.

This is the mindset I desire for you to have in completing this study book; a mindset that will seek and focus on what God has to say to YOU even if your friend is experiencing the *same season* at the *same time*. Please do not misunderstand me. I am not promoting separation from the Body of Christ or a self-centered lifestyle. I believe you will grasp and fully benefit from the lessons if you will have spiritual ears to hear what our Lord has to say to you, not comparing it to another. Let the Lord speak to you in your own season.

* * * * * * * * * *

As we view the seasons in *a new way*, we will be able to more effectively personalize these lessons. We know the winter season in Pennsylvania looks a lot different from the winter season in California. Likewise, you may be experiencing the same season as your friend, but it appears much different. Thus, it would be unwise to compare your particular season with that of another woman's, for each season is divinely unique as you are uniquely fashioned by our Creator. He alone knows the plans He has for you.

The word *comparison* is defined as the following:

The Exhaustive Concordance Of The Bible - **3850** παραβολή [*parabole* /par·ab·ol·**ay**/] n f. From 3846; **1** A placing of one thing by the side of another, juxtaposition, as of ships in battle.

Greek-English Lexicon Of The New Testament - **64.6** συγκρίνω[a]: to judge whether something is like something else—'to judge the degree of similarity, to compare.'

Merriam-Webster's Collegiate Dictionary - **com•par•i•son** \kəm-ˈpar-ə-sən\ *noun*

1 : The act or process of comparing: as
    a: the representing of one thing or person as similar to or like another
    b: an examination of two or more items to establish similarities and dissimilarities
2 : Identity of features: SIMILARITY ⟨several points of *comparison* between the two⟩

In your own words, write a definition of the word *comparison.*

Looking at the definitions above, how might you slip on the banana peel of comparison or competition (regarding your body, your lifestyle, your family, your achievements, your finances, your...)?

Read 2 Corinthians 10:12. What is our Father's opinion of those who compare themselves?

Much of my life has been wasted in comparison and it has taken me too long to refuse to be a victim of it any longer. How I wish that I would have learned what is revealed in the Word, for it would have saved me much heartache. We all observe one another as women. I am not talking about healthy observation wherein we learn and can improve. It's when comparison rears its monstrous head and you are left feeling angered or defeated by someone else's assumed advantage over you. Our culture promotes this very attitude to market products and anything that would give *you* the advantage over another.

How unwise it is to function like this on a daily basis since we do not have the capacity to make true comparisons. You see, only our all-knowing Lord is able to take two individuals and come up with a true conclusion that thoroughly covers all the facts. We, on the other hand, are limited in our fact finding and knowledge. How many young girls were deceived into thinking that Britney Spears had it all until they witnessed her life falling apart in the media? How many thought that Lady Diana had a fantasy life until her scandalous marriage was revealed? Ladies, we do not have the true capacity to compare ourselves with others. So let's decide right now to stop such a meaningless practice. As we proceed through this lesson, someone may be experiencing the same season as you, but be mindful that although you may experience some similarities, your season is unique.

Note the inadequate standards we use to compare, for our Lord's measurements are different from ours (Isaiah 55:8–9):

1. The church at Smyrna thought it was poor, but God said it was _____ (Rev. 2:8–9)

2. The church of the Laodiceans thought they were rich and wealthy, but God said they were_____ (Rev. 3:14–17).

3. The rich young ruler believed he had fulfilled all requirements to have eternal life, only to hear a difference of opinion by Jesus in verse 21. Read the account (Mark 10:17–22) and record below the difference of opinion and what resulted.

Another thing to note is that our Lord is not going to measure you on the basis of others' gifts or opportunities, only those which He has assigned to you (1 Cor. 3:11–15). Thus, our Lord does not compare you with another. Then why should you? Your body, your lifestyle, your family, your achievements, your finances, and all that pertains to you will be viewed according to His individual plan for you. This provides a way of *escape* and *freedom* from comparison to another. Of course, you will only know this for yourself if you choose to believe the Word over your next magazine article.

Even in regard to our Savior, He does not place a yoke of comparison upon us for we are already fully accepted and hidden in the Beloved. Read Ephesians 1:3–14. There is no condemnation once we have received Christ as Savior. The Holy Spirit, Himself, will take our inadequacies and complete the work He has already begun. We feel condemnation when WE compare ourselves with Christ—anyone would—for we all fall short (Romans 3:23)! Instead, when convicted of sin, we should confess and forsake it and give praise and thanks to Him for the things that are being conformed into His likeness, not fretting or distancing ourselves because we do not perfectly match up to Christ. We couldn't compare ourselves to Christ correctly if we wanted to, for even our viewpoint of Christ now is marred and incorrect. (See 1 Cor. 13:12.)

Having read the above, what insight have you gained in not relying on your ability to compare yourself to anyone?

The divine standard exemplified by Christ surpasses any human standards. Our Lord's evaluation is without fault. Praise Him for knowing you and your present season perfectly. Praise Him for being the only wise Judge who is able to evaluate you and your circumstances without error and still chooses not to compare you with anyone else.

Think about the waste of energy and time it takes to compare yourself with another. If you get plastic surgery on your face, it will still not be her face. If you purchase the same dress, it will still look different on you. Allow the Lord to free

> But "he who glories, let him glory in the LORD." For not he who commends himself is approved, but whom the Lord commends. (2 Corinthians 10:17–18 NKJV)

you from this bondage and unfulfilling way to spend your days.

Daily Divine Deliverance

Our Sovereign Lord has a wonderful plan for each one of us; expend your energy on following yours.

Take Time to Say a Personal Prayer of Deliverance.

SESSION 1
WEEK 1: Seeing Your Season

DAY 2: Seasons and Times

I went to my optometrist because I was experiencing a problem with my eyes. After he examined my eyes, I commented, "I don't know what could be wrong with my eyes. I've never had any problem with seeing before." He gingerly replied, "Mrs. Harris, your eyes are fine. What you are experiencing is a result of your age." I'm going to leave that alone and proceed with our lesson on seeing your season.

* * * * * * * * * * *

The Book of Ecclesiastes was written by Solomon, the younger son of David and Bathsheba. God made him a King in Jerusalem and the wisest man to ever live.

> Then Solomon said, "You have shown great loving-kindness to Your servant David my father, according as he walked before You in truth and righteousness and uprightness of heart toward You; and You have reserved for him this great loving-kindness, that You have given him a son to sit on his throne, as *it is* this day. "Now, O Lord my God, You have made Your servant king in place of my father David, yet I am but a little child; I do not know how to go out or come in. "Your servant is in the midst of Your people which You have chosen, a great people who are too many to be numbered or counted. "So give Your servant an understanding heart to judge Your people to discern between good and evil. For who is able to judge this great people of Yours?" It was pleasing in the sight of the Lord that Solomon had asked this thing. God said to him, "Because you have asked this thing and have not asked for yourself long life, nor have asked riches for

yourself, nor have you asked for the life of your enemies, but have asked for yourself discernment to understand justice, behold, I have done according to your words. Behold, I have given you a wise and discerning heart, so that there has been no one like you before you, nor shall one like you arise after you." (1 Kings 3:6–12 NASB)

Yet, as we have already discussed, man is inadequate to evaluate life as only God can do, for even Solomon, with all his wisdom, was led astray from the Lord his God (see 1 Kings 11:3–4). Without understanding the message of Ecclesiastes, it may appear to be a morbid book concluding that all is vanity. Nevertheless, it yields a harvest of wisdom for each season and the collection of times that make up each individual season.

Ecclesiastes 3:1 states, "To everything there is a <u>season</u>, a <u>time</u> for every purpose under heaven."

The Lord used Solomon to pen these words under the inspiration of the Holy Spirit. An understanding of the terms *season* and *time* will help us in our desire to glorify God in each season of our lives.

Defining terms -

(The words *season* and *time* may be interchangeable depending on the context in which the words are used.)

> ➢ **Season** – In Hebrew or Greek, no particular word designates season, but several words are used for a specific period of time described by such things as weather: the time of rain (Deut. 11:14), heat of summer (Ps. 32:4); features of the agricultural year: threshing and sowing (Lev. 26:5), blossoming of the fig tree (Matt. 24:32); or annual festivals: the Feast of

Unleavened Bread or Passover (Exod. 23:15; Luke 2:41; 22:1). [i] **related words** *period, term*

> **Time** – The Hebrews had their ways of measuring the passing of time (*CALENDAR) but the most frequent contexts for the words translated 'times' and 'seasons' suggest a concern for appointed times, the right time, the opportunity for some event or action. The commonest word is *'ēt* (*cf.* Ec. 3:1ff. for a characteristic use); *z*e*mān* has the same meaning. *mô'ēd* comes from a root meaning 'appoint' and is used of natural periods such as the new moon (*e.g.* Ps. 104:19) and of appointed festivals (*e.g.* Nu. 9:2). In particular, all these words are used to refer to the times appointed by God, the opportunities given by him (*e.g.* Dt. 11:14; Ps. 145:15; Is. 49:8; Je. 18:23). In NT the Gk. *kairos* often occurs in similar contexts, though it does not in itself mean 'decisive moment' (*cf.* Lk. 19:44; Acts 17:26; Tit. 1:3; 1 Pet. 1:11). [ii] **related words** *opportunity, proper moment*

If you are like me you might say, "Alright I have read the definitions, but how about making them plain and simple." So let's define the terms in a simplistic way that we may gain understanding.

Ecclesiastes 3:1 states, "To everything there is a season, a time for every purpose under heaven."

Season – duration: a ***period*** of time (cycle)

Time – smaller segment of measure: a ***point*** in time (the proper or appropriate time)

Every purpose has its time.

For example:

> ➤ There is the <u>season</u> or duration of a year. Within the year are smaller segments of <u>time</u>, called months.
> ➤ There is the <u>season</u> or duration of an hour. Within the hour are smaller segments of <u>time</u>, called minutes.
> ➤ There is the <u>season</u> or duration of one's life. Within that life are smaller segments of <u>time</u>, called daily events.

Just keep these definitions in mind for now. You will understand them better as we proceed through this lesson book.

Read Acts 1:4–8. The disciples have become anxious about knowing when Christ will establish His kingdom. What rebuke does Jesus give them about time and seasons?

Have you, like the disciples, believed the promise of God for your life, but were just a little bit inquisitive or impatient as to the time it would unfold? In what area of your life is that true today?

Looking at this same passage of Scripture, although we may not have insight into seasons and times, we are not left in the dark as to what our Lord would have us do presently. Although they were not given the answer to their question, what were they given and instructed to do?

Although you may not have all the answers right now, what do you presently know God would have you do? How will you step out in obedience and trust Him for the rest?

Read Ephesians 5:15–16. Looking at the following definitions (from NKJV), determine how you are redeeming the time. Are you walking wisely or foolishly in your season?

I am walking wisely ＿＿＿＿ I am walking foolishly ＿＿＿＿

See is *blepō* (βλεπω), "to discern mentally, observe, perceive, consider, contemplate, look to in the sense of taking care, take heed."

Circumspectly is *akribōs* (ἀκριβως), "exactly, accurately, and carefully."

Walk is *peripateō* (περιπατεω), "to order one's behavior, to conduct one's self."

Fools is *asophos* (ἀσοφος), "the unwise."

Redeeming is *exagorazō* (ἐξαγοραζω), "to buy up." *buying up the opportunity* "buy it back"—to use wisely the short time that believers do have.

Evil is not *kakos* (κακος), "evil in the abstract," but *ponēros* (πονηρος), "evil in active opposition to the good, pernicious."[iii]

We can all relate to being foolish at some time in our lives. I praise Jesus for being long-suffering toward us. Continuing in Ephesians 5, look at verses 17–21 and list some examples of what can be done to wisely redeem the time.

It is true that we do not know what a day may bring forth (James 4:13–17), but by living with a godly purpose and determination, the evil one will not be able to so easily derail us from the tracks of righteousness. Once the season and times have passed, they are irrecoverable—they cannot be recalled. Redeem and rescue your time out of the hands of that which would devour it: idleness, prayerlessness, excessive adorning of the body, worldly recreation, vain company, inappropriate sexual activity are all robbers of our time.

I had a desire to redecorate my living room. I believed the time would come when we would be able to do so. I created a design for the room in my mind in preparation for the day when it would take place. Since the Lord knew the precise time, I rested in that fact. Finally, the finances were available and my husband was willing to take extra days off to complete our project. I had to swing into action while the finances and manpower were available. In other words, I had to make the most of the opportunity to complete the room when it presented itself.

The two terms *seasons* and *time* are throughout God's Word. I praise Him for revealing that we do not need to compare our seasons with those of others—we do not know the details of our seasons and times, but God will guide us as to what we should do. As He does, we need to make the most of each opportunity given, knowing we live in a time where the days are short and full of evil.

> And He changes the times and the seasons; He removes kings and raises up kings; He gives wisdom to the wise, And knowledge to those who have understanding. (Daniel 2:21 NKJV)

Daily Divine Deliverance

The times and seasons of your life are precious. Redeem them for His glory and honor.

Take Time to Say a Personal Prayer of Deliverance.

SESSION 1
WEEK 1: Seeing Your Season

DAY 3: Spring and Summer

The seasons of the year mean different things to different people. Some enjoy the changing of the seasons, while others enjoy living in a steady and predicable climate without many surprises. I have a cousin who lives in Alaska, and while I could not imagine living in such a climate year in and year out, evidently she is doing just fine. For others, the changes in seasons mean a change in activities. Possibly the summer activities are more vigorous than those in the winter; and yet for some, the winter is more vigorous than the summer. Only a wondrous Creator could create such a massive group of individuals with such complex differences in one earthly place.

It's true of you, as a woman, your season may cycle in and out differently than your friend's. You may have a holding pattern within one season more than the others. The length of each season and the activities that take place within each is unique to you as well.

In the remainder of this session, you will see what season you are in presently by understanding how each season is described and by identifying similarities that match your circumstances today. Let's begin…

Spring

Spring is a season of *renewal*. Using your imagination, can you identify with any of the following points?

> _____ As new flowers sprout forth, you have a sense of renewal

> _____ You have a bright youthfulness about you

➢ _____ As a flower-bed, you are surrounded with many colorful choices

➢ _____ Maybe there's a new outlook, a new hairstyle, a new friendship, or a new undertaking

➢ _____ As refreshing rain, new opportunities have fallen upon you

➢ _____ Birds serenade you with songs of cheer

➢ _____ You're buzzing full of energy and believe you can conquer what lies ahead

➢ _____ You're smelling a bouquet of blessings

Ruth is an example of "Spring." Read Ruth 1:1–14. Then read the following passages and briefly write what is taking place in her life that denotes a time of gladness, new opportunities, renewal or beginnings.

Ruth 1:15–19 -

Ruth 1:22 -

Ruth 2:5–13 -

Ruth 4:13–22 -

I have chosen Ruth as an example of "Spring" for the abundance of renewal she experienced in spite of the many challenges she faced with the death of her husband. If you read the entire account of Ruth, you can see how she receives Naomi's God, the one true God Jehovah and leaves the false gods of Moab. She enters a new land, with new people and new customs during the time of a new harvest beginning. God rewards her with a new husband (Boaz), a new son (Obed) and a new privilege of being in the lineage of David and Christ our eternal King.

The "Spring" season then is a season of renewal, regeneration, rekindling, revitalization, rebirth, repair, replenishment, rejuvenation or restoration.

Are you in a season of "Spring?"

YES _____   NO _____

* * * * * * * * * * *

Summer

Summer is a time of *sadness*. Using your imagination, can you identify with any of the following points?

> ➤ _____ There is excessive heat in your life from which you would like to find some relief

> ➤ _____ You so desire to get away to a secluded place and quiet yourself as if on a beach, taking in the sounds of the ocean waves and seagulls.

> ➤ _____ You need an Olympic-size pool of encouragement for your soul

> ➤ _____ You may be sensing a need to shed your outer layers of phoniness and bear more of your true self to others

➤ _____ Your emotional air conditioning is broken

➤ _____ You feel like a lonely cactus in a dry desert place

➤ _____ You're more bitter than the lemons used for lemonade

➤ _____ Your internal radiator has overheated and you find yourself spewing off a lot of steam

Hagar is an example of "Summer." Read Genesis 16:1–5. Then read the following passages and briefly write what is taking place in her life that denotes a time of sadness, harshness, or affliction.

Genesis 16:6–9 -

Genesis 21:8–13 -

Genesis 21:14–16 -

Hagar is an example of "Summer" for there were times of sadness and desolation as a result of her and Ishmael acting in the flesh. If you read the entire account of Hagar, you will see how she has to submit to her mistress, Sarai/Sarah, even to the point of giving her body to bear this couple a son. She is pregnant when she is first expelled from camp. The second time, she and her son are both expelled from the camp. They both find themselves in the desert, without water, and ready to succumb to death. Her hopes and dreams of being Abraham's special wife and having her son be heir to everything, melt away with the desert heat that evaporates the very life out of her body.

I would be negligent not to mention how God graciously rescued Hagar and her son in the midst of her affliction. I can testify of His grace towards me in the summer seasons of my life. He even multiplied Ishmael's seed as He did that of the promised son, Isaac. However, as pointed out in Galatians 4:21–31, the two women and their sons are representative of the two covenants of God. Hagar and Ishmael are representative of the flesh and bondage, while Sarah and Isaac are representative of the Spirit and freedom.

The "Summer" season then is a season of sadness, grief, affliction, depression, sorrow, misery, despondency, woe, unhappiness or gloom.

Are you in a season of "Summer?"

YES _____ NO _____

If you are not able to identify fully with one of these two seasons, it's fine. We have two more to explain that we may identify and see what your season is.

> Then God said, "Let there be lights in the firmament of the heavens to divide the day from the night; and let them be for signs and seasons, and for days and years.
> (Genesis 1:14 NKJV)

Daily Divine Deliverance

How funny is it that our <u>Immutable</u> God should create seasons that change? You are truly blessed not to be stuck in one season for the rest of your life.

Take Time to Say a Personal Prayer of Deliverance.

23

SESSION 1
WEEK 1: Seeing Your Season

DAY 4: Autumn and Winter

What a delight it was to be reunited with my Aunt Ruth after being separated from her since my childhood. She is not really my aunt, but my mother's cousin. She reminded me of my deceased mother with her joyful disposition. The thing that tickled me the most was her expression, "Go away from here!" We have not had contact for ages, but you can hear me say at any time, "Get out of here!" I use that expression when I'm excited about something. One time a person really thought I was telling them to leave. My visit with her will be etched upon my heart forever. She's eighty years old, but baked me a cake and gave me a black-and-white picture of my mother and her when they were young. A long season of having lost contact had come to an end. She told me before I left, "Baby, now that we have found each other, I will not let you go."

Isn't God like that? We love Him because He first loved us (1 John 4:19). Now that He has redeemed us, He will not let us go.

* * * * * * * * * * *

<u>Autumn</u>

Autumn is a season of *change/transition*. Using your imagination, can you identify with any of the following points?

> _____ As Autumn foliage, change is taking place in your life

> _____ As a tree with its leaves, you're slowly dropping and letting go of what used to be

> _____ It's harvest time and you are beginning to enjoy your crop

➤ _____ You're getting prepared and not afraid of what winter may bring

➤ _____ Like pilgrims past, thankfulness and praise are in your heart

➤ _____ You can snuggle up, feel safe and secure in spite of...

➤ _____ Cider, spiced cookies, pumpkin pie—it doesn't matter, you're learning contentment

➤ _____ Daylight is shortening, but you are getting stronger as you adjust

Esther is an example of "Autumn." Read Esther 1–2:4. Then read the following passages and briefly write what is taking place in her life that denotes a time of change or transition.

Esther 2:7 -

Esther 2:8–9 -

Esther 2:15–18 -

Esther Chapter 4 -

Of course, we have only touched on a few verses of this fascinating story of Esther and how God used her for that very time to deliver her people the Jews. As we read about Esther, it's easy to see why she is chosen as an example of change and transition. She goes from her parents' home to her uncle Mordecai's home; her surroundings change from familiar to foreign as she moves to the king's palace; from a lowly position to a charming queen over 127 provinces from India to Ethiopia (vs. 1); and from security to risking her life for her people. Whew, how much more can one person take? Life can present a roller-coaster of transitions that can even include, as noted in Chapter 4, a change or transition of our mindset.

The "Autumn" season then is a season of change, transition, adjustment, moving, switching, alteration, modification, revision or transformation.

Are you in a season of "Autumn?"

YES _____   NO _____

* * * * * * * * * * *

Winter

Winter is a time of *stillness*. Using your imagination, can you identify with any of the following points?

➤ _____ As a hibernating bear, you are cozy and settled in

➤ _____ The elements outside are harsh and you may not go as much as you used to

➤ _____ While others complain about the fallen snow in their lives, you see its glistening beauty

➤ _____ Much like a fireplace, others seem to draw close to the heat of your love

26

- ➢ _____ The aroma of home is a delight
- ➢ _____ You are wrapped in the warmth of others' kindness
- ➢ _____ You realize there is new growth underneath the frozen ground of your situation
- ➢ _____ Joy keeps floating to the top like marshmallows in hot cocoa

Anna is an example of "Winter." Read Luke 2:36–38. Then write below what is taking place in her life that denotes a time of stillness.

Anna had lived seven years with her husband and was a widow for eighty-four years. The earliest age for marriage was probably twelve years old, so it is likely that she was at least 103 years old during this account in the temple. Widows were often neglected and exploited, but she served God night and day waiting for the appearance of God's promised Messiah. She quietly and patiently waited upon God, trusting, believing, knowing, expecting and anticipating while not fretting or striving to work things out. She was still. Anna, being a prophetess, joined in with Simeon, announcing to all who were looking forward to the redemption of Jerusalem that the Messiah had come!

The "Winter" season then is a season of stillness, tranquility, calmness, serenity, immobility, silence, quietness, composure or peace of mind.

Are you in a season of "Winter?"

YES _____   NO _____

I trust you have narrowed your choices down to one season. As mentioned before, it's a blessing that we cycle in and out of seasons and are not stuck in one forever. Nevertheless, God is a very present help in each season and desires to lavish His love upon you even now.

> While the earth remaineth, seedtime and harvest, and cold and heat, and summer and winter, and day and night shall not cease. (Genesis 8:22 KJV)

Daily Divine Deliverance

Jesus is aware of your season and invites you to know His peace and joy. Do you believe this?

Take Time to Say a Personal Prayer of Deliverance.

SESSION 1
WEEK 1: Seeing Your Season

DAY 5: Seasons and Christ

At the time of this writing, I am coming out of a season of "Summer." I had received a phone call telling me that my oldest brother, Chuckie, was at the hospital emergency room. His condition was so bad that the nurse asked if I wanted to return him to the nursing facility with hospice or go ahead and admit him to the hospital. I was speechless, for I had just spoken with an individual from the nursing facility the day before and received a report that he was doing well. I called because he would always call me daily, and I had not heard from him. The words of the nurse began to smother any breath of hope I had for him recovering, but I decided to have him admitted to the hospital. I tried to remain hopeful that Chuckie would walk out the hospital as he had often walked out before in situations like this.

Being the only girl with four brothers (two older and two younger), I informed my other brothers of what had taken place. My next oldest brother was able to leave his job and drive to Pennsylvania that same day. After returning from the hospital, getting settled for the night and making sure my husband and brother were taken care of, I collapsed into my bed.

Piercing the silence in the early morning hours, the phone rang and I could see by the caller ID that it was the hospital. The words that poured into my ears were hard to receive; I was told to rush to the hospital because they did not expect Chuckie to make it. Upon arriving at the hospital and seeing how his condition had deteriorated from the day before, I began to pray for God's will concerning my brother. All but one brother was able to make it to the hospital before witnessing Chuckie taking his last breath. My father and mother had been deceased for many years, and to see my sibling depart made my heart ache in a way I had not felt for quite some time.

The love and intimacy I have with our Lord provided the comfort I needed. Having His indwelling Spirit and the surrounding love of my husband, family, church body and friends kept me through those days of adjusting to my brother not calling daily.

I praise Jesus for His sovereign love toward us. We are able to get to know Him in a way that even death's sting is temporary. Even when we're standing on a sure foundation of doctrinal truth concerning death, He understands our tears and emptiness when separated from a loved one. After all, Jesus was momentarily separated from His Father on our behalf and is able to identify with all of our afflictions (Heb. 4:15). We truly have a Savior that knows what it is to be touched by the Spring, Summer, Autumn and Winter seasons.

Let's take a moment and see how the seasons may be applied to different areas of Jesus' life. Match the Scripture with the season by connecting them with a line.

Matthew 4:1–11	Winter
Mark 4:35–41	Autumn
John 2:1–11	Summer
Luke 24:50–53	Spring

We read of the scorching "Summer" season of Jesus in His testing by the devil. We are able to witness His "Winter" season in sleeping in the midst of the ferocious storm on a cushion and finally calming the storm and fears of the disciples. We see "Spring" in the making of the new wine at the wedding and this being the beginning of miracles that Jesus performed, manifesting his glory and producing faith in his disciples (John 2:11). The season of "Autumn" is obvious when He blesses the disciples and departs from them and is carried up into heaven.

Remember, we randomly go in and out of these seasons. Choose *one* of the passages below and identify it with a season, and then explain why you believe it describes that particular season in Jesus' life.

Mark 9:2–8
Matthew 14:22–27
John 12:3–8
Luke 22:45–48
John 19:28–30, 33

I believe_____ (Scripture) describes a

_____ season in Jesus' life, because_____

_____

_____

_____

Hebrews 2:14–18 NIV states:

> Since the children have flesh and blood, he too shared in their humanity so that by his death he might destroy him who holds the power of death—that is, the devil—and free those who all their lives were held in slavery by their fear of death. For surely it is not angels he helps, but Abraham's descendants. For this reason he had to be made like his brothers in every way, in order that he might become a merciful and faithful high priest in service to God, and that he might make atonement for the sins of the people. Because he himself suffered when he was tempted, he is able to help those who are being tempted.

How does the fact that Jesus identifies with you and knows what it is like to be in your season bring comfort and encouragement to you?

Looking at where you are today, what season did you decide is taking place in your life right now? Even if you are experiencing a time of transition, choose which season is the dominant of the two for this discussion.

- ❑ Spring
- ❑ Summer
- ❑ Autumn
- ❑ Winter

How did you come to this conclusion in light of the seasons' descriptions given earlier? In other words, what did you see in the description that you could relate to?

What is the most challenging part of this season?

When Jesus was transfigured before Peter, James and John, the sight of His countenance and the Father bearing witness from the cloud was too much for them (see Matthew 17:1–8). They fell on their faces in fear. I rejoice over what the Scriptures stated next, "But Jesus came and touched them and said, 'Arise, and do not be afraid.' When they had lifted up their eyes, they saw no one but Jesus only." I'm ready to jump up out of this chair!

Whatever you are facing at this moment in your season, it has not escaped the awareness of our Lord! He does not want you to be afraid! He has experienced it all and will help you! But here's the thing...you need to lift up your eyes and see only Jesus—not the problem, not the pain, not the unknown, not the solution...ONLY JESUS! He is with you and has your situation under His sovereign control! Get your focus back on Him! He is your way maker, your strong tower, your healer, your deliverer, your peace, your strength, your provider, your protection...oh my, there's not enough paper left to describe what He is to you in this season of your life. Ask Him to give you eyes to see His transfigured presence in the midst of your current season. I can attest to the fact that He is faithful and will do it. Whew, let me calm down.

Having a better understanding of the *seasons*, let's dig deeper to determine the *times* of the seasons in our next set of lessons.

> Does He not see my ways, and count all my steps? (Job 31:4 NKJV)

Daily Divine Deliverance

If I were to ask you to tell me your season, what would you say? And if I were to ask you where Jesus is, what would you say?

Take Time to Say a Personal Prayer of Deliverance.

SESSION 2
WEEK 2: Struggles in Your Season

DAY 1: Struggles in Ecclesiastes 3:2–3

A mother can pretty much understand what her toddler is saying even when no one else does. This was true of me with my three sons; however, I struggled a little when it came to my three grandchildren learning to form words. I had to listen intently to decipher exactly what they were saying. At times, I noticed their frustration as they tried to get Mom-Mom to understand.

Do you find yourself struggling at times to hear and understand the voice of God? Can it be that you are easily distracted by many things and you need to listen more intently?

In this session, we will focus on examples of "times" that take place within a "season." We will then go further by identifying at least one specific "time" that is taking place in your life right now. Ask the Lord to remove the wax from your spiritual ears that you may clearly hear what He is saying to you through this session.

* * * * * * * * * *

Remember what was covered in our last session. Ecclesiastes, Chapter 3:1 states:

To everything there is a <u>season</u>, a <u>time</u> for every purpose under heaven.

In this verse, we see that ***everything*** (nothing excluded) has a "season" and a "time." Every activity and purpose of man has its proper "season" (duration) and "time" (a point in time). The NIV switches these terms in its passage.

The Bible Knowledge Commentary states the following: Solomon followed his general statement with a poem on 14 opposites (given in Ecclesiastes 3:2–8), each of which happens in its time. The fact that Solomon utilized polar opposites in a multiple of seven and began his list with birth and death is highly significant. The number seven suggests the idea of completeness and the use of polar opposites—a well-known poetical device called merism—suggests totality (Ps. 139:2–3). Though the exact meaning of some of these "activities" is uncertain, Solomon intended to affirm that *all* a person's activities, both constructive and destructive, and *all* his responses to people, objects and events happen in their times.

So the "times" included in the next seven verses are an illustration of one's total life, from the time they are born to the time they die. These "times" are presented in sets of opposites, the positive and negative activities (depending on your translation, it may say "purposes" or "desires.").

I will refer to these activities as *struggles*. If you look up the word *struggle* in a thesaurus, you will see words such as *resist, fight back, great effort, exertion* and *battle*. So in this session, we will look at some of the ways we must resist, fight back or battle within our seasons. Job 14:1 states, "Man *who is* born of woman is of few days and full of trouble." Although we must battle to live righteously and to not give into temptation, Jesus died that we would have an abundant life. We need not fear, for John 10:10 states, "The thief does not come except to steal, and to kill, and to destroy. I have come that they may have life, and that they may have *it* more abundantly." Two opposites indeed!

You have identified your season. As we go through the next seven verses in this session, let the Holy Spirit help you narrow the choices down to *one* "time" that is a struggle for you. Even if He brings several to the forefront, focus on one at a time so that you are not overwhelmed. In the following session, we will find "Strength in Your Season" for that particular struggle and any future struggles you may face. As always, prayerfully ask our Lord to give you wisdom as we proceed through Ecclesiastes, Chapter 3.

Verse 2: *A time to be born, And a time to die;*
A time to plant, And a time to pluck what is planted;

Note the Hebrew Poetic Opposites:

A time to be born   ↔   a time to die
A time to plant   ↔   a time to pluck what is planted

From this passage, we see that there is a time to be born and a time to die. We have no control over when we are born or when we die. The times in-between, however, do allow us the opportunity to make many choices.

Planting seeds and plucking weeds are a must if a harvest is to be reaped. The same is true of life. There are some things that must be planted and others uprooted if one's life is to be abundant.

Can it be that this is the *time* for you to:

> ➤ Start doing some small deed that is good
>   (e.g. Maybe send that card, make that phone call, etc.)

> ➤ Uproot or stop doing that which is not producing any good
>   (e.g. Possibly deciding not to participate in gossip.)

Note times of planting (starting) or plucking (stopping) in the following Scriptures:

Hebrews 13:16 -

Luke 6:33–36 -

James 1:19–20 -

Proverbs 2:21–22 -

What is God saying to you personally about the "times" given in Ecclesiastes 3:2?

Vs. 3 *A time to kill, And a time to heal;*
    A time to break down, And a time to build up;

Note the Hebrew Poetic Opposites:

| A time to kill | ↔ | a time to heal |
| A time to break down | ↔ | a time to build up |

Ladies, this is not condoning premeditated murder. Sometimes wrong or evil must be resisted with force, and other times, healing is the goal. Also, it may be time to break down the negative aspects of your life and build up the positive ones.

<u>Can it be that this is the *time* for you to:</u>

> ➤ Forcefully kill all thoughts that tear you down
> (e.g. I am worthless, I cannot do this, I should be married by now...)

> ➤ Start the healing with thoughts that build you up
> (e.g. I am complete in Christ; I can do all things through Christ who strengthens me...)

Note times of breaking down or building up in the following Scriptures:

Jude 20 -

Acts 20:32 -

Revelation 9:20–21 -

Judges 2:1–4 -

What is God saying to you personally about the "times" given in Ecclesiastes 3:3?

Struggles may not be a lot of fun, but they are a vital part of our spiritual growth and maturity.

> But recall the former days in which, after you were illuminated, you endured a great struggle with sufferings. (Hebrews 10:32 NKJV)

Daily Divine Deliverance

Sunshine and rain, joys and sorrows;
do you see how both are beneficial?

Take Time to Say a Personal Prayer of Deliverance.

SESSION 2
WEEK 2: Struggles in Your Season

DAY 2: Struggles in Ecclesiastes 3:4–5

I had the opportunity to speak at a women's retreat where I met a woman who sheepishly pulled me aside to tell me her story. To make a long story short, from the time she was a little girl, she was reprimanded by her mother whenever she cried. As a result, she hated to see other women cry or fall apart emotionally. It really irritated her. She hesitated to attend retreats for that reason. Nevertheless, after the last session of the day, to her own amazement, she came forward with tears flowing down her face. The Spirit of the Lord had overwhelmed her and set her free. My tears were mingled with hers as we embraced and praised God together.

* * * * * * * * * * *

Vs. 4 *A time to weep, And a time to laugh;*
   A time to mourn, And a time to dance;

<u>Note the Hebrew Poetic Opposites:</u>

| A time to weep | ↔ | a time to laugh |
| A time to mourn | ↔ | a time to dance |

Solomon covers the range of emotions, both private and public, in these lines of the poem. The Hebrew words for *weep* and *laugh* indicate expressions of an *individual's emotions* while the Hebrew words for *mourn* and *dance* indicate expressions of a *group's emotions*. In other words, there is a time for an individual to be sad and a time for a person to be happy. There is a time for an individual to join others in lament and a time for that person to join others in a good time.

Can it be that this is the *time* for you to:

> ➢ Stop stuffing your grief, let it out, cry and cry some more (e.g. Even if you are a leader in church or ministry, you allow yourself to be a real person whether crying over another's death, another's falling away from Christ, one's own sin, etc.)

> ➢ Now that you are over your sadness, it's time to laugh again (e.g. Give yourself permission to bathe in the joy of the Lord, allowing Him to wash you clean of all grief.)

Note times of weeping or laughing in the following Scriptures:

Luke 6:21 -

1 Peter 1:6–9 -

Genesis 45:3–5, & 14–15 -

Psalm 73:21–24 -

What is God saying to you personally about the "times" given in Ecclesiastes 3:4?

Vs. 5 *A time to cast away stones, And a time to gather stones; A time to embrace, And a time to refrain from embracing;*

Note the Hebrew Poetic Opposites:

A time to cast away stones	↔	a time to gather stones
A time to embrace	↔	a time to refrain from embracing

There are various interpretations of these lines. They are believed to deal with friendship and enmity. We gather stones to build walls to keep others out. We scatter stones to tear down walls to make peace with others. So there is a time to show affection and a time to refrain from showing affection.

Can it be that this is the *time* for you to:

➢ Forgive and let that person back into your life
   (e.g. When you build walls to keep others out, you actually imprison yourself.)

➢ Leave that person alone and get help
   (e.g. Maybe there is an individual who is not good for you or is leading you away from God.)

43

Note times of embracing or refraining in the following Scriptures:

Genesis 32:11 & 33:1–4 -

Ephesians 4:32 -

2 Chronicles 7:21–22 -

Luke 17:3 -

What is God saying to you personally about the "times" given in Ecclesiastes 3:5?

During the times when I have taught this lesson to groups of women, it was a serious time of reflection. For some the tears fell, while for others the shackles fell.

> Therefore if the Son makes you free, you shall be free indeed. (John 8:36 NKJV)

Daily Divine Deliverance

If you have a willing heart, these struggles can be diminished by the power of His indwelling Spirit.

Take Time to Say a Personal Prayer of Deliverance.

SESSION 2
WEEK 2: Struggles in Your Season

DAY 3: Struggles in Ecclesiastes 3:6–7

I cannot believe how many specialty coffee shops there are in my area. The menu for coffee is the same as that of a fancy restaurant with numerous selections. I have to admit that I had the best cup of coffee when William and I went out to dine for our anniversary. It was a caramel-mocha blend with whipped cream on top. It was such a treat, since I do not drink coffee often. Years ago, when I did drink a lot of coffee, even ice coffee, there were basically one or two flavors. Today, there are numerous options. I know people who struggle to get on their feet in the morning until they have their coffee. They drink coffee each day. Evidently, there are many who need a jumpstart, for the coffee shops are booming! Are you in a slump and need a "pick me up?" I wish I could extend my arm out to where you are and at least give you a cup of encouragement. I pray that you will not despair and that your struggles will be transformed into puddles so they will roll off of you like water off a duck's back. Did I hear someone shout…Quack! Quack!

* * * * * * * * * * *

Vs. 6 *A time to gain, And a time to lose;*
A time to keep, And a time to throw away;

Note the Hebrew Poetic Opposites:

| A time to gain | ↔ | a time to lose |
| A time to keep | ↔ | a time to throw away |

There comes a time to accumulate (hold on to) and a time to get rid of possessions, friendships, goals or whatever. However, that is not to say that we should be greedy, stingy or self-centered.

Can it be that this is the *time* for you to:

> ➢ Do something that will bring enjoyment to you
> (e.g. Take a trip, join a group or class, get a pedicure, etc.)

> ➢ Give something away to bring gladness to someone else
> (e.g. Give away those clothes that have been hanging in
> your closet that are practically new, but you rarely wear.)

Note times of gaining or losing in the following Scriptures:

Proverbs 1:19 -

Matthew 25:6–10 -

Isaiah 31:6–7 -

Revelation 16:15 -

What is God saying to you personally about the "times" given in Ecclesiastes 3:6?

Vs. 7 *A time to tear, And a time to sew;*
A time to keep silence, And a time to speak;

Note the Hebrew Poetic Opposites:

A time to tear   ↔   a time to sew
A time to keep silence   ↔   a time to speak

This refers most likely to the ancient custom of tearing one's clothes in grief. If so, as in verse 4, it's both a time to express and a time to recover from grief. Sometimes by not keeping silent we cause grief. There is a time to remain quiet and a time to voice our opinion; a time to listen and a time to remark. Life and death are in the power of the tongue (Prov. 18:21). Isn't it amazing that God put the tongue behind two gates: the lips and the teeth! However, there comes a time when you must speak or you will implode internally.

Can it be that this is the *time* for you to:

➢ Stop speaking in a way that tears down or grieves others? (e.g. Refuse to allow the stench from the gutter of your mind to invade others' lives.)

➢ Open your mouth and say what is necessary to mend things with another. (e.g. Can you speak a few words that will change another person's day or entire life?)

Note times of silence or speaking in the following Scriptures:

Proverbs 11:13 -

Titus 3:1–2 -

Proverbs 31:9 -

Ezekiel 29:18–21 –

What is God saying to you personally about the "times" given in Ecclesiastes 3:7?

We are getting there, ladies. One more verse to cover in reference to the "times" found within the season of life and death.

> Our soul has escaped as a bird from the snare of the fowlers; The snare is broken, and we have escaped. (Psalm 124:7 NKJV)

Daily Divine Deliverance

Remember the beginning story of this lesson?
Are the puddles starting to form?

Take Time to Say a Personal Prayer of Deliverance.

SESSION 2
WEEK 2: Struggles in Your Season

DAY 4: Struggles in Ecclesiastes 3:8

My husband and I went through a season of struggle with a pair of birds that had built a nest in one of the bushes in our driveway. You may wonder why this would be a struggle? Well, every time our cars were in or near the driveway, the birds would proceed to fight the enemy bird in our side rearview mirrors. They would bang so hard into our mirrors trying to get this perceived enemy that I thought their beaks would break. They were so engaged in their fight that they would leave feathers and droppings on the mirror, side windows and down the side of our cars. We couldn't believe that such little birds could have such large tanks. It was gross to see. We found the only way we could stop them was to cover our mirrors with plastic bags, and even then they would be on the car trying to get at the mirror inside. So we had to pass this tip on to our neighbors and anyone who parked near our house because these birds weren't playing around. They had a love for their offspring in the nest, but a hate for any perceived bird that would invade their territory.

* * * * * * * * * * *

Vs. 8 *A time to love, And a time to hate;*
A time of war, And a time of peace.

Note the Hebrew Poetic Opposites:

A time to love	↔	a time to hate
A time of war	↔	a time of peace

This part of the poem reads differently and gave me a bit of struggle in trying to understand it. When we look at love and hatred, we must be careful how both emotions are exercised. If enlarged, hate can lead to war while love can lead to peace. Love

50

and hate appear to refer to that which is personal, while war and peace appear to refer to that which is on a national level. Now concerning its poetic form, Paul stressed Christians are to love what is good and hate what is evil (Rom. 12:9). Do we instead love what is warring against us and hate what would lead to peace?

Can it be that this is the *time* for you to:

➢ Cease **loving** what is *warring* against your Spirit (e.g. End a relationship that is pulling you further and further away from the body of Christ.)

➢ Cease **hating** what is your true source of *peace* (e.g. God has disappointed you, so you cease reading His Word and praying.)

Note times of love or hate in the following Scriptures:

Psalm 45:7 -

Psalm 97:10 -

James 4:1–3 -

Romans 14:14–18 -

What is God saying to you personally about the "times" given in Ecclesiastes 3:8?

This morning, I was looking out the open window smelling the fresh air and enjoying the scenery before any cars or people began to stir in my neighborhood. I enjoy speaking with my Father very early in the morning and have come to treasure these sacred moments. This morning, I saw Him rouse the leaves of the tree; I heard Him sing melodiously through a bird; I saw His radiance in the rising sun; and I felt Him in the very breath I took. My soul rose up in Hallelujahs and praise!

As we journey through the seasons of life, may we yield our souls continuously to our Maker and enjoy sweet communion with Him. If our soul is in a summer season, may we drink of His unfailing love. He can melt away all despondency and rejuvenate us with His loving care. If our soul is in an autumn season, may we trust Him and not be ruled by sight. He is an inerrant Father and not even capable of making mistakes. If our soul is in a winter season, may we find rest in Him. For in the stillness and silence, He is secretly preparing new shoots and new growth from any bulbs of fatigue. The repose is as necessary as the activity. If our soul is in a spring season, may we display His resurrection power. For He alone is able to take that which was dead and make it alive; to take that which was old and make it new; and to take closed doors and burst them wide open. *(I just want to put exclamation points after all these sentences!)*

Write out the following Scriptures in a <u>one-sentence</u> prayer of your own:

Psalm 33:20 -

Psalm 130:5 -

Psalm 143:11 -

Psalm 94:19 -

Psalm 103:1 -

Now that you have reviewed Ecclesiastes 3:1–8, choose one of these verses that best describes a struggle you are experiencing. I would like for you to choose **one**, even if there are several, so you may not be overwhelmed in completing the next session's material.

I have chosen verse _____ as my "time"
of struggle during this season of my life.

We have concluded our focus on some of the "times" that take place within the "season" of life—the "times" between birth and death. We have witnessed within these "times" some struggles that we may face. In Session 3, we will focus on the

> In the multitude of my anxieties within me, Your comforts delight my soul. (Psalm 94:19 NKJV)

strength our Savior provides to be victorious over these struggles.

Daily Divine Deliverance

What is more dominant in your heart today—love or hate?

Take Time to Say a Personal Prayer of Deliverance.

SESSION 2
WEEK 2: Struggles in Your Season

DAY 5: My Times Are In Your Hand

Write out Psalm 31:14–15 -

Isn't it amazing (except for The New International Version) that this verse does not say "hands"? It specifically says "hand" in the majority of translations. It's not like "You are in good hands with Allstate."

This touched me deeply because I have a burgundy leather chair in my office and it's my meeting place each morning with God. After I spend time reading His Word and fellowshipping with Him, I get on my knees and place my upper body in the cushion of this chair. The chair has seaming on the upper and lower part that resembles to me the lines in the palm of a hand. So each morning before I go about my day, I picture myself in the palm of His hand as I pray. I bear my soul as I intimately commune with Him curled up in His Almighty Hand; note that I said "hand."

What's also fascinating in this verse is that my "times" (plural) are in His "hand" (singular). He is so awesome that He does not even need both hands to intercede on my behalf. Now I know that God is Spirit and that He does not actually have one or two hands, but He gives us this picture so we can understand and comprehend Him better.

Think of this. When you place your pocketbook on your shoulder, do you use one or both hands? When you style your hair, do you use one or both hands? When you push a shopping cart up and down the aisles, do you use one or both hands? When you tightly embrace, do you use one or both hands? When you pick up a baby, do you use one or both hands? Get my point?! Yet, the very weighty things and struggles that enter our lives do not diffuse the *tiniest measure of His strength*. The issue comes back to the preceding lines; is the Lord our God and do we trust Him?

All of our "times" are in God's hand. A cross-reference to this verse is in Job. Read Job 14:5.

What do you believe this verse is saying?

It is clear that the "times" of our lives are set by God and we cannot go beyond their limit. The years, months, days, hours, minutes and seconds are known by Him. By His tender mercy, I believe He does not reveal this to us. Otherwise, we may have a mental breakdown or heart attack if we had this information. Even if He knows that He has decided to extend our days, He's still in control and not us. Read 2 Kings 20:1–6. What did God do for Hezekiah?

What instruction are we given in Deuteronomy 30:19–20?

Choose life, ladies! Our times and their limits are in His hand. Yes, we may experience struggles along our journey, but we will see as we continue this lesson book that we need not be defeated by them. A chick hatching from an egg, a butterfly from a chrysalis, and a baby from the womb of its mother all experience momentary struggles. Ah, but on the other end of their struggles is beautiful life and victory!

Let's close this session by looking at one more verse. Please read Hebrews 4:14–16.

Record below at least three blessings noted in these verses that you have received from Christ:

1.

2.

3.

Praises to our High Priest, the Son of God!

> Wait on the LORD, And keep His way, And He shall exalt you to inherit the land; When the wicked are cut off, you shall see it. (Psalm 37:34 NKJV)

Daily Divine Deliverance

Which is flowing through your spiritual veins—life or death?

Take Time to Say a Personal Prayer of Deliverance.

SESSION 3
WEEK 3: Strength for Your Season

DAY 1: The Source of Our Strength

Two of the original members of the old Motown singing group *The Delfonics* are related to me. During my youth, I can remember all the excitement of their being a part of the Motown sound. In 1970, they came out with a song entitled, "Didn't I Blow Your Mind This Time?" For whatever reason, this title came to mind when I was reflecting upon the source of our strength. The source of our strength is God! He continuously blows my mind with His supreme power over the enemy. The fact that He abides in me and delivers me from the fiery darts of the enemy is beyond my comprehension. I believe the thing that blows my mind the most is something that I heard and would like to share with you:

> You cannot do anything to make God love you less,
> You cannot do anything to make God love you more,
> His love for you is *complete, unconditional,* and *unchanging*!

Doesn't that blow your mind?

* * * * * * * * * * *

In our last lesson, we identified a "time" or struggle that we are dealing with in our season. We know that each season has its own joys and sorrows. We may laugh or weep, love or hate, plant or uproot along our journey. Now in this session, we would like to gain strength to overcome this struggle and any future struggles that we may face.

Repeatedly in the Word of God we are told about the source of our strength. God is the source of our strength! God is greater and stronger than any struggle we may face! Since this is true, He is able to produce in us the necessary strength needed to overcome whatever we may face on any given day. If you will acknowledge your weakness and turn to Him for strength, He will not forsake you. Instead, He will give you the victory over your struggle. He doesn't have to, but He desires to prove His strength in your situation so that you may trust Him and have no doubt. Read 2 Chronicles 16:9 below:

> *For the eyes of the LORD run to and fro throughout the whole earth, to show Himself **strong** on behalf of those whose heart is loyal to Him.*

Let's look at other Scriptures that confirm God is the source of our strength. Jot down any thoughts you may have next to the Scripture reference.

Psalm 46:1 –

The word *refuge* means to flee to safety and to find shelter and protection from danger and distress. A picture of this is given in the Old Testament. There were six Levitical cities designated for people to find refuge if they had accidentally caused the death of another (Joshua 20:7–9). These cities were a place of refuge where the individual could find asylum from any avengers of the dead until the case could be judged by the elders. If the person was found to be innocent of deliberate murder, he or she could remain in the city of refuge and find safety (Num. 35:6–28; Deut. 19:1–13). God is portrayed as our refuge in this Scripture and others (see Psalm 9:9). Are you screaming out for a place of refuge in your current struggle?

The word *strength* means quality or the state of being strong; mighty; healthy; to be able; strong enough to; to enable; to empower; to become capable; and power to resist. If you are to have strength to overcome any struggle in whatever season you are facing, you must turn to Jesus and **ask** Him to give you strength (look at the definition again). Call upon Him the very moment you sense a struggle erupting in your life. Should you decide to go forth in your own strength, you will fall flat on your face. I am sure we can all attest to times when we have hit the ground and had a mouthful of dirt.

The word *help* means to give assistance or support; to make more pleasant or bearable; to relieve; to change for the better; to deliver or save; to further, advance or promote; to be on hand to aid; and to restrain from doing something. The fact that He is a "very present help" means that He is always abundantly available to help in times of trouble.

Now look at these three words again and what they mean. If God were to provide any of these three things for you right now in the midst of your struggle, would it prove to be a source of strength?

Let's continue to receive encouragement and jot down our thoughts:

Psalm 68:35 -

Psalm 18:32 -

Psalm 27:1 -

Psalm 18:1–2 -

Note the word *my* and how often it is repeated in the last two verses. This is a personal proclamation. Now say these two verses out loud replacing each "my" with your own name.

Without a shadow of a doubt, we can see by these few Scriptures that God is our strength! This means that when we look to Him, He will make us strong enough, empower us, help us to be capable, and even give us the power to resist when needed. However, should we decide to handle our struggles in our own strength, He will not interfere. He has given us the freedom to choose our way or His way. Yet, when we seek, ask, or call upon Him for strength, He will be there for us.

Look at Philippians 4:13. What is possible when we have Jesus as our source of strength?

Now read Ephesians 6:10–13 NIV:

> Finally, be strong in the Lord and in his mighty power. Put on the full armor of God so that you can take your stand against the devil's schemes. For our struggle is not against flesh and blood, but against the rulers, against the authorities, against the powers of this dark world and against the spiritual

forces of evil in the heavenly realms. Therefore put on the full armor of God, so that when the day of evil comes, you may be able to stand your ground, and after you have done everything, to stand.

More than likely, according to this verse, what are you struggling against?

According to this verse, how are we able to be strong or have strength to resist and stand in the evil day?

The Lord Jesus Christ makes us strong and provides the strength we need to fight against Satan and all that he can bring against us. In our next lesson, we will talk more about this spiritual war.

> The Lord is their strength, And He is the saving refuge of His anointed. (Psalm 28:8 NKJV)

Daily Divine Deliverance

Has this struggle made you weak? To Whom will you turn?

Take Time to Say a Personal Prayer of Deliverance.

SESSION 3
WEEK 3: Strength for Your Season

DAY 2: Strength to Demolish Strongholds

Although there are some that may choose not to own one, the majority of homes have at least one computer. These computers can store an amazing amount of data and recall any information when requested. Today's computers are more advanced than the typewriters of yesterday. When you consider the functions of each, there is no comparison. Likewise, our brains can store an amazing amount of data and can recall information in a matter of seconds. I know there may be a woman right now who feels her brain has retreated back to being a typewriter. Even in this, my dear, you can be strong.

* * * * * * * * * * *

In this lesson, I would like to share just *one* way the Lord gives us strength. He gives us strength for our season by demolishing strongholds. Read 2 Corinthians 10:3–5.

Paul is using military terms in this Scripture. Any Christian that lives upon this earth will find that they are involved in a spiritual war. We are in a *war* and each side has weapons. We are not playing patty cake with each other. No one goes to war to sit down and have a social gathering. You go to war to stop or, if necessary, destroy the enemy. The purpose of weapons is to kill the other side (see John 10:10)!

We need to recognize:

1. Read 2 Corinthians 10:3. The *war* is taking place in our minds. Read Romans 7:15–25.

   Our old way of living before receiving Christ may be referred to as the sinful nature. The sinful nature loves to do evil, which is the opposite of what the Holy Spirit desires in a Christian. Similarly, the Spirit gives us desires that are opposite from what the sinful nature desires. These two forces are constantly fighting each other, and our choices are affected by this conflict.

2. Read 2 Corinthians 10:4. Our *enemy* is not flesh and blood. Read Ephesians 6:12.

We may walk around here in the flesh, but our weapons are not carnal or of the flesh. There are times when we want to look at other people as the problem or cause of our struggles. It is important to look beyond the physical person and see what has taken place spiritually. Is the person a tool of Satan to discourage or harm me? Look beyond the person to the true source.

3. The head of the other army is Satan, and his *weapons* are lies. Read John 8:44.

When we accept any lie of Satan and believe it as truth, we are standing on dangerous ground. For this lie can easily be developed into a stronghold. I will explain later what a stronghold is.

4. Of course, the head of our army is the Lord Jesus Christ! We have a whole list of weapons, and our armor is described in Ephesians 6:10–18 (please read). Our major weapon is truth— the Word of God. By abiding in the Word and <u>knowing</u> the truth, we will have divine power (NIV), mighty through God (NKJV), to demolish strongholds (see 2 Corinthians 10:4 again).

By His divine power, Jesus Christ has already won the war! We are members of His army, so we too have the victory! His mighty power is able to destroy any stronghold the enemy may erect against us. Knowing that the war is already won should cause us to have courage when faced with any battle that may confront us until we go home to be with Him. The battle may appear intense, but remember, the war is already won!

The war that we face is within and is not fought with fleshly weapons. It is a war between whether we are controlled by the truth of God or the lies of Satan. The lies of Satan can actually become strongholds if not brought under the divine power of Christ. Let's take a moment to understand what is meant by stronghold.

A "stronghold" is a fortified place. Basically, a stronghold is the fortification around and defense of a lie that <u>you believe</u>. When the Word says stronghold, it means it! This lie has a <u>STRONG</u> <u>HOLD</u> upon you. These fortified lies cannot be penetrated **without divine weaponry**. We need not fear because in our previous lesson, we found that God will exercise His mighty strength on behalf of His children. This is important because this lie blocks you from knowing God's will as He is the God of all truth.

God's Word clarifies even more what these strongholds are. Read 2 Corinthians 10:5.

These strongholds are arguments, pretensions, imaginations, or speculations (depending on your Bible translation) that are set up against the knowledge of God, but they are not true.

> **Arguments** – a reason given in proof or rebuttal

> **Pretense** – a claim made or implied; especially one not supported by fact

> **Imaginations** –the act of creating mental images of what has never been experienced

> **Speculate** – to take to be true on the basis of insufficient evidence

We have a stronghold when we take something to be true on the basis of insufficient evidence or what we have imagined. We come to conclusions without actual facts. Then we are tormented by this false belief.

Looking at verse 5 again, how do we gain the victory over any stronghold?

You will experience the victory when all opposing thoughts are taken captive to the obedience of Jesus Christ. He is the chief of police who captures and locks up every criminal thought that is a lie. Any lie that tries to exalt itself *above* the knowledge of God must be cast down and taken captive. We cannot do this in our own strength. It can only be done by divine power or the strength of God!

Truth triumphs over lies! When we bring all our imaginations, lies, and arguments before Christ and seek His truth, we will see Him demolish our strongholds. We have to be willing to face the truth about others, our situations, and ourselves. When we accept the truth revealed by God, it shatters the stronghold! We will have to continue to do this repeatedly until we are no longer prone to the lie we have held onto for so long.

Another bad thing about strongholds is if you hold onto them for long periods of time, they have a way of multiplying. They incubate! Get rid of lies right away! Find out the truth!

In this section of *Strength for Your Season*, you will have more reading than questions to answer so you may concentrate on the essentials of the war in defeating strongholds. You may think that you are not involved in this spiritual war, but you are. No one gets to sit on the sidelines and be inactive. Either you are adhering to the truth of God or the deceiving lies of Satan. There is no middle ground.

In the upcoming lessons, I will take examples from my own life to help you understand further how the strength of the Lord is

> And you shall know the truth, and the truth shall make you free. (John 8:32 NKJV)

available to us to demolish strongholds. At the end of the session, you will understand better how to have His strength to overcome any struggle you may face in the seasons of life.

Daily Divine Deliverance

Have you ever believed what Satan said
over what God said?

Take Time to Say a Personal Prayer of Deliverance.

SESSION 3
WEEK 3: Strength for Your Season

DAY 3: The Root of the Matter

Remember, I am concentrating on just *one* key area whereby the strength of God can be manifested in our lives. There are so many more; however, we will focus on His strength in demolishing strongholds. By the end of this session, you will agree that this was a good choice in addressing any struggle that we may face. If you will grab hold of what is being said, you will begin to quickly gain strength for your season.

God is making me more sensitive to lies, arguments, and imaginations that take place in my thoughts. I am realizing more and more that strongholds have the ability to keep me from walking in truth and knowing God more. If you have a creative mind and imagination as I do, you must constantly allow Jesus to bring all wrong thoughts into His captivity. I no longer walk around ignorant of Satan's devices to imprison me by his lies.

Let me share one example from my life. I had a stronghold regarding suffering. I believed if you were obedient to God, you would experience His blessings and not suffering. I lived as obediently as I could, but God began to allow me to experience suffering. It caused me to question His love. If He loved me, why would He let me suffer?

I believed that if you were obedient to God, you would not suffer. This is a lie! (Read 2 Timothy 3:12 and Philippians 1:29.) This lie was reinforced and became a stronghold by the teaching I received and by fellowshipping with those who held this mindset. Whenever someone would experience a trial, they would question what that person did wrong. This mindset is portrayed in the Book of Job when his friends believed his suffering was a result of some sin in his life. Therefore, not only did I believe this lie, but it became a stronghold that affected the lives of my children. I taught

67

them that if they would do good things, good things would happen to them. If they did bad things, bad things would happen to them. As they grew older, they found that this was not true. They began to see that they could do what was right and suffer for it. They saw others do wrong and appear to be rewarded for it. It began to make them question both God's goodness and love. Anything that is *partially* true is a lie! The truth does not contain a little error; truth is absolutely true! Job was righteous and upright, but suffered. Psalm 37 mentions that evil men do prosper, even if it is for a season. Many of us are holding onto things that sound good, but are not Biblical at all. And what is worse is we are passing them onto our children! It wasn't until we believed and accepted the truth of God concerning suffering that this stronghold was shattered like glass. Let's be careful, ladies, that we do not pass our strongholds onto our children or future generations.

Now after studying His Word, I understood the lie that I accepted, believed, and had reinforced. In accordance with the Bible, God's reasons for suffering are many. Nevertheless, one thing I have come to appreciate about suffering as a Christian is that it surfaces and exposes impurities in my life. If I respond correctly to suffering, it will prove my faith genuine and produce spiritual growth in my life (see 1 Peter 1:7). In other words, the truth is that Christians do suffer even when they are obedient. The actual suffering, when responded to correctly, will cause us to be identified with and conformed into the image of Christ. Christ's willingness to suffer on our behalf proved His love is genuine towards us, and our willingness to suffer on His behalf proves our love for Him to be genuine as well. I do not want to get sidetracked into an extensive study on suffering, for our focus is on strongholds and how to obtain the strength to overcome them. My point here is how my accepting a lie developed into a stronghold, not only for me, but also for my children.

Note the following passages about suffering and write at least two blessings that result in the life of Christians who suffer.

1 Peter 5:10   Revelation 2:10   Romans 8:18

Blessings:

(1)

(2)

Read 2 Corinthians 1:3–5 NASB below and then (1) describe what God provides in the midst of your suffering, and (2) describe the positive effect suffering has on you and others.

> Blessed *be* the God and Father of our Lord Jesus Christ, the Father of mercies and God of all comfort, who comforts us in all our affliction so that we will be able to comfort those who are in any affliction with the comfort with which we ourselves are comforted by God. For just as the sufferings of Christ are ours in abundance, so also our comfort is abundant through Christ.

(1)

(2)

In all honesty, I have come to appreciate what suffering produces in my life. Of course, it's not fun to experience suffering when it is taking place. Yet, when dealt with in the strength Jesus provides, it results in blessings not only for us, but for others. We are able to comfort them with the same comfort Jesus provided for us when we experienced suffering. I have learned to not ask "why," but "what?" What is it that I am to learn from this, Lord? I fight against the stronghold of doubting God's love for me. I can actually see His provision and love as He brings me through each situation. My mind has been changed regarding suffering and the stronghold has been demolished by His divine power.

You will know if you have a stronghold because the same emotions or thoughts will surface repeatedly in a particular area. The same hurt or pain is rehearsed over and over again. The reason it keeps surfacing is because you have not dealt with the lie completely. Oh, you may have dealt with some issues on the surface as a result of the stronghold, but you have not pinpointed the root of the stronghold. You must deal with the root of your stronghold, the main lie that keeps you defeated. We all know that if you just cut off the top of a weed and don't pull out its root, it will grow again. The same is true of a stronghold; you must acknowledge the lie when exposed, but you must uproot it completely to be free of it.

I will demonstrate what I mean. As I spent time in God's Word, He exposed the lie of my questioning His love for me when He allowed me to suffer. However, He did not stop there. He went deeper and exposed the root of the lie that was fortified in my life. The root lie was, "All suffering is a result of sin." So naturally I thought if I was suffering, then I must displease God. If I displeased God, then I concluded He would not love me. No one can walk in the freedom of God's love while carrying the burden of displeasing Him. Over and over again, this lie was fortified by others and by the teaching that I believed. It took years of studying the Scriptures to be fully free of this stronghold (remember a <u>strong</u> <u>hold</u>).

I believe if you really want to know the truth, God will show you. He cannot lie and has said in His Word that He has given us the Holy Spirit who will lead us into *all* truth (see John 16:13). However, it takes quiet time before Him in prayer and the reading His Word. At times it may take God using a Christian counselor or friend to come alongside you to point out lies that have taken root.

Call upon Him for help and be sensitive to His leading. He will deliver you!

I believe Satan's big weapon against Christians is keeping us too busy to spend time with God. This is the only way lies are exposed and we come to know Him and His truth. Some of the ways we will know God's truth and increase in strength is by doing the following tasks. Take a little inventory right now and place a check beside the things you are doing to defeat the fortified lies of the enemy.

- ➤ Pray consistently
- ➤ Read the Word of God daily
- ➤ Go to church regularly
- ➤ Participate in a Bible study
- ➤ Believe and trust God even though you don't understand
- ➤ Be honest and tell the truth; do not cover your sin—get delivered from it
- ➤ Forgive and not hold grudges

This was not given to place the burden of guilt upon you. Look at them as guidelines of things to do that you may be delivered

> Trust in the LORD forever, For in YAH, the LORD, *is* everlasting strength. (Isaiah 26:4 NKJV)

from strongholds and have strength in the seasons of your life.

Daily Divine Deliverance

Are you willing to have any strongholds revealed?

Take Time to Say a Personal Prayer of Deliverance.

71

SESSION 3
WEEK 3: Strength for Your Season

DAY 4: The Old Flesh

One morning I was in the shower just enjoying the refreshing water and sweet aroma of the soap, when something dark caught my eye. Near my foot was a cricket the size of King Kong! (At least it appeared that big to me.) My reaction to this unexpected visitor caused a tidal wave in the bathroom. Where did he come from? How did he get into our house? Have you ever asked the same question about a thought that popped into your head out of nowhere? Have you ever been on your knees praying and suddenly have a crazy thought? Have you ever asked yourself, where did that come from?

* * * * * * * * * * *

You know what I have come to realize? Much of the Christian life includes God exposing or bringing to the surface lies we have believed, having us acknowledge them, destroy them by accepting His truth, and then understand and know him to a higher degree because we no longer hold onto these false beliefs. This is how we are constantly made into the image of His Son. Our old self (lies and all) are constantly put to death, and He is constantly being made alive in us as we walk in His truth (see Galatians 2:20). The old self was our mindset and way of living before we received Jesus as Savior. We know anything that is dead does not move or have any control. This is a painful process. We do not like to get paper cuts much less have this part of our life put to death. Jesus did not only have the strength and power to conquer death, He triumphed over sin during his life on earth. Likewise, anything that is trying to enslave us must be put to death by Christ. He desires to provide the strength we need to be liberated as well. What a merciful Savior!

Please take a moment to read Romans 6:1–14 NLT below:

> Well then, should we keep on sinning so that God can show us more and more of his wonderful grace? Of course not! Since we have died to sin, how can we continue to live in it? Or have you forgotten that when we were joined with Christ Jesus in baptism, we joined him in his death? For we died and were buried with Christ by baptism. And just as Christ was raised from the dead by the glorious power of the Father, now we also may live new lives. Since we have been united with him in his death, we will also be raised to life as he was. We know that our old sinful selves were crucified with Christ so that sin might lose its power in our lives. We are no longer slaves to sin. For when we died with Christ we were set free from the power of sin. And since we died with Christ, we know we will also live with him. We are sure of this because Christ was raised from the dead, and he will never die again. Death no longer has any power over him. When he died, he died once to break the power of sin. But now that he lives, he lives for the glory of God. So you also should consider yourselves to be dead to the power of sin and alive to God through Christ Jesus. Do not let sin control the way you live; do not give in to sinful desires. Do not let any part of your body become an instrument of evil to serve sin. Instead, give yourselves completely to God, for you were dead, but now you have new life. So use your whole body as an instrument to do what is right for the glory of God. Sin is no longer your master, for you no longer live under the requirements of the law. Instead, you live under the freedom of God's grace.

We see by reading these passages in Romans that we have left that old way of living and entered a new way of life once we receive

Jesus as our Savior. We also see that Jesus has given us strength to conquer sin. Any sinful struggle or stronghold is included in this. Look at the word *sin* throughout this passage and explain how the power of sin has been put to death in your life.

Read Ephesians 4:21–24. Since the truth is in Jesus and we are instructed to be renewed in the spirit of our mind, what are *we* to put off and put on? What does the "old" and "new" represent?

I would like to give you additional examples of rooting out strongholds so you may be renewed in the spirit of your mind.

Let's say someone appears to be looking your way, you speak, and they do not answer. As a result, you may wonder why they did not speak. A second time, the same events occur, and now you are upset and begin to believe that that person is angry or deliberately not speaking with you. A few other things happen that fortify this lie. It is a conviction of yours that this person has some grievance against you. You can continue down this trail or you can approach the person face to face to find out the truth. You may find out that the person had a burden on her heart and was not truly concentrating, so she did not see you. A number of things could be true besides what you were thinking. The fact is you will not know the real truth until you approach that person and discuss the matter. You do not find the truth by calling someone else on the phone or bringing a third party into the picture just to spew out your hurt. It is always better to keep the situation one on one with the individual you are having the misunderstanding with. After all, only they know the truth, not someone else who was not involved at all. Once you have confronted the person in love, you will know what to do next by the response you receive. At least you will know the truth and not expend any further energy spinning thoughts around in your mind. Be practical—there are times when reconciliation will take place and there are also times when it may not. In both situations, God is still on the throne.

My middle son played football at Penn State and we had great fun tailgating with other parents and friends. Then my youngest son played football at the University of Virginia and the tailgating was organized differently than what we were used to. Tailgating is when you fellowship over food before the game begins. Each time we purposed to meet the other parents at the Virginia stadium to tailgate, something would delay us with our drive from Pennsylvania, and we would not make it in time. This happened several times to the point that I began to believe a lie. I believed the other parents must have thought that we were snobbish and had no desire to fellowship with them. At the games, parents had a special section in which to sit. There were things that took place even in our section that reinforced this lie, and I began to feel that many of the other parents had a negative opinion about us. Then finally, one day the Lord reprimanded me for not finding out the truth. So when I sat down next to one of the moms, I proceeded to explain how our family was having a hard time trying to make the tailgating before the game. She said, "Oh, Paula, we live right here in Virginia, and we don't make them either." That truth pumped the stronghold right from my heart and any feelings of being misunderstood by the other parents were vanquished. At the root of this lie I believed that the majority of the families were making it and had noticed that we attended once or twice. This was not true!

I cannot emphasize it enough—the sooner you find out the truth, the sooner you can walk in freedom and not be held hostage by your old fleshly ways. Once you know the truth, you can respond in the strength provided by Jesus. Additionally, you can confess any sin of believing a lie and in that instance put the old fleshly ways to death. Whenever that thought or reasoning tries to resurface, you call on Christ and remember what He has to say about the matter. You decide to believe Jesus over the lie!

What about you? Could there be a stronghold of...

o God is not love because He has allowed something to happen to you

o You cannot go on living because of the loss of your spouse

o Your parents divorced so you will never be able to marry and truly be happy

o You did not accomplished something so you are a failure

o Several people are saying bad things about you so you reason something is wrong with you

o God did not protect the people in the twin towers so how can you expect Him to take care of you

Is the Holy Spirit surfacing a stronghold in your life? What lie has been fortified in your life?

It's only in facing the truth that you can be set free. This truth is revealed by our Heavenly Father through His Divine Word. It is not revealed through our emotions or feelings.

> For the law was given through Moses, but grace and truth came through Jesus Christ. (John 1:17 NKJV)

Daily Divine Deliverance

What step do you need to take to find out the truth?

Take Time to Say a Personal Prayer of Deliverance.

SESSION 3
WEEK 3: Strength for Your Season

DAY 5: Truth Triumphs

I cannot speak for you, but even though I know God **cannot** lie, I am not always so ready to agree with or believe His words concerning me. Oh, I can quickly believe His truths for others, but when those promises are pointed in my direction, I have to pause and take them in. Even my name, Paula, means "little" and at times I have to fight being overtaken by a small mentality that renders me spiritually incapacitated. This small mentality says "I can't" more than "I can." This mentality regarding myself is not honoring to God. So I stay before Him for daily strength to defeat wrong thinking and demolish any emerging strongholds. Proverbs 23:7 lets us know that as a person thinks in his heart, so is he. Our thoughts turn into beliefs, our beliefs govern our decisions, and our decisions direct our lives. It's amazing how something as little as a thought can create gigantic results! You are not what you think you are, but what you think…***you are***!

* * * * * * * * * * *

You may have seen the words for *Success* on a plaque in the bookstore. They are:

> *If you think you are beaten, you are. If you think you dare not, you don't. If you'd like to win, but think you can't, it's almost a cinch you won't. If you think you'll lose, you're lost, for out in the world we find, success begins with a person's faith; it's all in the state of mind. Life's battles don't always go to the stronger or faster hand, they go to the one who trusts in God and always thinks "I CAN." (Author unknown)*

Overall, what is your mentality?

I CAN! _____   I CAN'T! _____

In our last lesson from the Book of Ephesians, Chapter 4, we read that we are to be renewed in the spirit of your mind. Read Romans 12:1–2. According to this verse, our lives are changed or transformed by something happening to our minds. What needs to happen to our minds?

Look at Titus 3:5, and put a check next to the correct statement.

_____ By determination I can bring about this renewal in my life.

_____ The renewal in my life is the work of the Holy Spirit.

Again, I believe the spiritual warfare of the Christian life is God exposing or bringing to the surface lies we have believed, having us acknowledge them, destroying them by accepting His truth, and then understanding and knowing him to a higher degree because we no longer hold onto these false beliefs. The more this becomes a lifestyle, the more you will have strength in the seasons of life.

Let's go through these steps. Be thorough and honest as you proceed, and you will know a peace and freedom that only God's Spirit can provide.

STEPS FOR STRENGTH IN YOUR SEASON

1. We are in a spiritual warfare and the battle begins in your mind. Has God revealed a lie that has been fortified in your life? (Perhaps the struggle that you identified has caused you to turn away from God's truth.)

2. Acknowledge your belief of a lie and confess this before the Lord. Ask Him to deliver you from any strongholds or struggles as a result.

3. Destroy the lie by accepting God's truth. You do this by taking the lie you acknowledged and matching it with some truth found in God's Word. Believe what God has said about it. If you do not know how to use the topical index or concordance of your Bible to locate Scriptures, seek the help of a mature Christian or Pastor who can assist you. Here are some examples of lies.

LIES	TRUTH THAT DEFEATS THEM
I am a failure!	Romans 5:6–11; Romans 8:37
God will never forgive me for what I did!	Read 1 John 1:9; Romans 8:1
I can't do this!	Philippians 4:13; Psalm 27:1
I don't know what to do!	Proverbs 2:3–6; James 1:5

4. Understand and know Him to a higher degree because you are no longer holding onto these false beliefs. Remember the guidelines given on Day 3 so you can develop a consistent walk with Jesus.

5. Praise Him for deliverance and continue to be on the alert for when God reveals any lies you may have taken to be true. What do the following passages tell you regarding your mindset?

Colossians 3:1–4 -

Philippians 4:6–8 -

If you will grab hold of this section, you will quickly begin to gain strength for your season. Pray to God that you may not be ignorant of Satan's devices used against you. Look below at some seasonal lies that must be defeated.

- ➢ Spring (Season of Gladness) – **Lie**: Any Christian who is mature will experience this season continually. **Truth**: James 1:2–4 We must wake up! There are three other seasons to go through and all are for your benefit.

- ➢ Summer (Season of Sadness) – **Lie:** Once you develop a dry area in your life, it will never flourish again. **Truth:** 2 Corinthians 9:8 Grass may be brown as hay one day and become a vibrant green the next due to a rain shower.

- ➢ Autumn (Season of Change) – **Lie:** God is with me, but this transition is just too hard. **Truth:** 2 Corinthians 2:14 Whenever you follow Him, He will not orchestrate your defeat, but your victory. It is said that God will allow you to go through the troubled waters; not to drown you, but to cleanse you.

- ➢ Winter (Season of Stillness) – **Lie:** Things are great! I can kick up my heels and finally become complacent. **Truth:** 1 Peter 5:8–9 Bears can hibernate because of the fat stored up, but sooner or later they have to come out and be replenished. You will need to always be prepared for the next season.

As children of God, we are not left alone in our times of struggles or weaknesses. One major thing we can do to have strength for any season is to demolish strongholds by the divine power of Jesus that dwells within us. This is going to take our being alert and submissive to the Spirit's leading in our lives. This is a process of sanctification whereby we are set apart for God. We cannot afford to ignore any false thing that enters our minds, especially if it is a reoccurring mindset that is causing us to be defeated. It's only in facing the truth that we can be set free. John 17:17 states, "Sanctify them by Your truth. Your Word is truth." Truth triumphs over lies!

Take a moment to read Isaiah 40:28–31. What hope does this give you concerning the struggles in your life?

I would like to close this session with 1 Peter 5:10–11. "But may the God of all grace, who called us to His eternal glory by Christ Jesus, after you have suffered a while, perfect, establish, **strengthen**, and settle you. To Him be the glory and the dominion forever and ever. Amen."

> ...In quietness *(spending time alone with Me)* and confidence *(relying on My sufficiency)* shall be your strength. (Isaiah 30:15 NKJV - Italics mine)

Daily Divine Deliverance

Can you reflect on a past victory that
will strengthen you today?

Take Time to Say a Personal Prayer of Deliverance.

SESSION 4
WEEK 4: Savoring Your Season

DAY 1: Beautiful in Its Time

Newscasters reported the frantic wedding planning for the date of 07-07-07 because many brides believed it to be the luckiest day of the century. There was a frenzy to find open dates for caterers, reception halls and ministers! I had to chuckle since my wedding anniversary this year fell on 07-13-07, known as Friday the 13th. I guess these women would say, "What in the world was she thinking? What woman would not have figured out that her anniversary could fall on that date?" I do not hold the same view as the world does concerning this date. However, I would agree that my thinking and life were messed up before my heart became wholeheartedly His. My husband and I have been together for thirty-four years and are growing stronger each year by the grace of God! I delight, take pleasure in, and savor the years we've been together. I'm so happy that our Lord does not get weary, for I have required a lot of work. God has taken a messed-up couple and a messed-up date (according to the world) and made it beautiful over time.

* * * * * * * * * * *

To savor your season means to enjoy, take pleasure in, and value the season you are experiencing at the present time. When you savor your season, you accept and appreciate it regardless of what is taking place. God directs us on how to do this in the remaining passages of Ecclesiastes, Chapter 3.

To Savor Your Season:

1. Know that God makes everything beautiful in its time (vs. 11, 16–17)

2. He has put eternity in our hearts (vs. 9–11)

3. We cannot find out God's works from beginning to end, so we may revere Him (vs. 11, 18–21 & 14–15)

4. Rejoice, do good, enjoy what we labored for—it is the gift of God (vs. 12–13 & 22)

I would normally have the opportunity to explain these four points at a retreat in one session. However, in this lesson material it will be spread over a five-day period. They are so intertwined that I prayed the cohesiveness of what is being said would not be lost. My Father, I thank You that my mouse of concern is nothing for Your eagle eye as You guide my penning of this material.

Know That God Makes Everything Beautiful In Its Time

Today you may feel overwhelmed by life; for example, children or boss' demands, creating a home, trying to get pregnant, carpooling, paying bills, cleaning the house, cooking, hoping to get married, hoping you'll get that job, or maybe developing a close friendship. Our Father is more than able to take the black coal of our lives and make it into beautiful diamonds. You may ask, "But when?" The answer is recorded in verse 11.

Read Ecclesiastes 3:11 and write when God will do this for you.

In His providential plans and control, God has an appropriate time for every activity. The cold of winter has its own beauty, the heat of summer another, the black beauty of night and the bright brilliance of day another, and even wrong being made right.

When we dissect this verse further, we gain additional insight:

God – Our creator, ruler, sovereign king, lover of our souls, provider, protector, righteous Judge…

Has made/hath made – past tense; it's already done! He has taken the necessary items and has already made; it is finished…

Everything – *Everything*! Not one thing missing, not one thing overlooked, not one thing neglected; He has complete control…

Beautiful – appropriate, proper, of value, of full bloom or development, good, pleasant, agreeable, excellent…

In its time/in His time – in its right time; in the timing that fulfills His plan and His will for you; in the timing that pleases Him…

You see that the word *beautiful* does not refer to outward attraction or adoring. Instead, the beauty lies in it being the appropriate or proper timing of God. It's similar to when God created the world, stepped back, and then concluded, "It was very good" (Gen. 1:31). His creation was beautiful in His sight.

To savor your season, I recommend that you commit this passage to your mind and heart by repeating it as often as needed. Chew over it as a cow its cud. I know that's not a pretty picture—chewing something, swallowing it, and then regurgitating it to chew it and start the process all over again. However, when we mediate on the Word of God, this is exactly what we are doing. We are taking the Word of God, spiritually digesting it, and then deliberately pondering it over and over again until it actually becomes a part of our character and living.

Should you get discouraged concerning your wayward husband, children, or friend, remember this verse. When it appears that you are laboring in vain or some injustice is taking place concerning you, remember this verse. There's something freeing in knowing that God sees all and will make *everything* right in His time.

Ecclesiastes 3:16–17 gives additional information. Summarize what it says below:

Were you abandoned by your parents? Have you ever been sexually, verbally or physically abused? Were you left by your husband with mouths to feed? Did your church family let you down? Were you taken to court unjustly? Are you constantly being misunderstood? Did you flee to a source to find justice only to experience injustice?

Read what Jeremiah had to say to God about injustice in the world in Jeremiah 12:1. What were his observations?

Going back to Ecclesiastes 3:16, what did Solomon observe?

With the wisdom God gave Solomon, what did He conclude about God in Ecclesiastes 3:17?

What did Asaph conclude in Psalm 73?

Have you observed the injustices of our day and wondered why divine judgment has been delayed?

How can God be in control when there is so much evil in our world, and it appears the wicked get away with their sin and the righteous seem to suffer in their obedience? God's Word lets us know that God has a time for everything. He is working out His eternal plan, even with the ability to use the evil deeds of men. His timing for judgment here and after death is just and beautiful (appropriate and proper).

The issue of evil and injustice thriving has to do with all of us as fallen human beings. People are evil and do evil deeds. You can take the nicest person and if exposed, you can see that they sinned by having a bad thought, wrong motivation, or neglecting to do some good along the way. Every time we put clothes on our backs, it should remind us that God had to kill an animal to cover Adam and Eve's nakedness after they sinned against Him in the garden. He had made everything beautiful and given them all that they needed (they didn't even need to shop for clothes). However, they doubted Him and sin entered the world. Let's be specific...sin entered us! Now if we are left to ourselves, we will think and do all sorts of evil. We don't have to be taught how, it just comes naturally. What we need to escape this evil fate is to ask Jesus Christ to save us and supernaturally receive His strength to overcome the evil that is in us and this world. Not only do all of us need to wear clothes now, but we will all stand before God one day and be judged whether we have or have not received Jesus as Savior and Lord. If necessary, stop now and read the Afterword in the back of the book to make sure you have done this.

I used to teach a Bible study for women at our county prison, but I also had the clearance to go up on the cellblock where they lived. One time as I was going from cell to cell to minister to the women, my eyes fell on this frail figure with prominent white hair and quiet demeanor. Here this old woman had written bad checks to get things for her grandchildren and was now sitting in prison. That day my heart sank as I started my car to drive away, for I had to leave this sweet grandmother behind.

None of us want to face the fact that we have sin crouching inside waiting for an opportunity to pounce forward. Only Christ can deliver us from the jaws of evil and make us pure and righteous.

Are the righteous judged the same as the wicked? Read the accounts below and write your opinion in the space provided.

Read Matthew 13:40–43 -

Read Genesis 18:16–33 -

Read Romans 2:5–11 –

Once we have placed our faith in Jesus Christ and He has restored us to fellowship with the Father and given us eternal life, nothing and no one is able to snatch us out of His loving arms. Read John 10:27–30 and Romans 8:38–39.

Although everyone who has received Jesus as Savior need not be fearful about being judged as the wicked, we will be judged for something else. We will be judged for what we have done with our life and all that God has given us to possess. Did we use it for our own desires or for His desires? Do all the seasons of our life display a heart for worldly things or a heart for God? We will not lose our salvation, but we may lose our rewards. Matthew Henry stated, "The world has not only gained possession of the heart, but has formed prejudices there against the beauty of God's works."

So we know that God is working out His eternal plan in spite of the deeds of evil men and the injustices that take place upon the earth. His plan will not be stopped, but carried out to the end when He shall make all things beautiful in its time.

> I know that you can do all things; no plan of yours can be thwarted. (Job 42:2 NIV)

Daily Divine Deliverance

The Righteous Judge is ready to plead your case.
Have you given it to Him?

Take Time to Say a Personal Prayer of Deliverance.

SESSION 4
WEEK 4: Savoring Your Season

DAY 2: Eternity in Our Hearts

Have you ever wondered why all people, regardless of nationality or geographical location, have a god or gods? Even those who claim to be atheists are, in reality, setting themselves up to be their own god or unknowingly believe in a religion of humanism. Why isn't it that only one country would have some way of acknowledging a higher power? Instead, why do we find this throughout history and across the world? We see in the Old Testament that men would even carve a god out of wood and worship it. Where is this drive coming from and why would such an act make sense to anyone?

* * * * * * * * * * *

<u>He Has Put Eternity In Your Heart</u>

Read Isaiah 46:3–11 and Jeremiah, Chapter 10, and jot down the differences between other gods and the One True God, Jehovah.

MAN-MADE GODS	ONE TRUE GOD, JEHOVAH

What are some of the man-made gods we serve today? How do they compare with the One True God, Jehovah?

What is the most frightening god of all that man can worship? Read Ezekiel 28:2 and Daniel 4:30–33.

Anything that we exalt above God is an idol or god to us. We can even set ourselves up to be our own god. That is why Ecclesiastes 3:11 is of utmost importance to us. This verse lets us know that the One True God has **put** (NKJV) or **set** (KJV, NAS, NIV) eternity in our hearts. What does this mean? Let's look at some definitions and answer that question. A full definition of these words would take several pages to explain, but I will present enough of a summary for our understanding in this lesson.

ETERNITY - (olam; eon; Greek equivalent, aion, aionios, aidios) As finite beings, we cannot comprehend eternity. Eternity is not measured by time, yet an eternity apart from time is an impossible conception. Eternity is not to be defined in terms of time, for an eternal existence is no more described by the notion of a present than by a past or a future. Time is purely relative, but eternity is not. So eternity is an unlimited, incalculable, continuous existence or duration that cannot be measured. Yet the eternity of God brings into harmony with itself the limitations and conditions of the temporal as described in the following Scriptures.

Isaiah 57:15 states, "For thus says the High and Lofty One who inhabits eternity, whose name *is* Holy: "I dwell in the high and holy *place,* with him *who* has a contrite and humble spirit, to revive the spirit of the humble, and to revive the heart of the contrite ones." Then Acts 17:27–28 states, "…He is not far from each one of us: for in Him we live, and move, and have our being…"

HEART - (lebh, lebhabh; Greek kardia) - According to the Bible, the heart is the center not only of spiritual activity, but of all the operations of human life. "Heart" and "soul" are often used interchangeably (Deut. 6:5; 26:16; comp. Mat. 22:37; Mark 12:30, 33). As the central organ in the body, forming a focus for its vital action, it has come to stand for man himself: his moral, spiritual, and intellectual life; also his emotions, passions, and appetites (Gen. 18:5; Lev. 19:17; Ps. 104:15). The heart is naturally wicked (Gen. 8:21), hence it contaminates the whole life and character of man (Mat. 12:34; 15:18; comp. Ecc. 8:11; Ps 73:7). Thus, the heart must be changed and regenerated (Eze. 36:26; 11:19; Ps. 51:10–14) before a man can willingly obey God.

Now that you have this understanding, in your own words write what you believe the passage means ("God has set eternity in their hearts.").

God is eternal and without measurement. We were made in His image and likeness (Gen. 1:26). This verse helps us to know that we were made for eternity, and the things of time cannot fully or permanently satisfy our hearts. Now read Ecclesiastes 3:9–10. This is Solomon's observation as he looks upon man and what takes place upon the earth. A paraphrase of these verses might read:

What permanence or lasting profit can a man
expect from the various types of labor in
which he is involved? He labors to gain, but it
is hard to find. God has given man this burden
for importance or significance.

We can now understand why a man in the far reaches of a deserted island would build a replica of God to worship. God has set eternity in his heart! He is aware that something exists beyond this world, but will not know God unless he surrenders to the work of the Spirit upon his heart. Here then is the "task" or "burden" of verse 10. Man has a capacity for eternal things and realizes that this life cannot be all there is. Yet, sin has corrupted his eternal perspective and will. Thus, he is in continual frustration: he yearns and works for eternity's fulfillment and yet does not know the Eternal One.

How does this work out in our lives today? If we observe people, we will see a continual frustration in their labors. People know something more exists beyond this world; but without God, they are unable to grasp fully what it is. We see people changing spouses, changing jobs, leaving families, leaving churches, leaving towns, and leaving godly principles just to possibly find what is missing. *We see a continual yearning for something more or better*. Many get married and wonder if their true soul mate (as if there was one) is out there somewhere in the abyss. The advertising and marketing agencies feed off of this pursuit. A woman may be born with one color of hair and crave for a different color (ouch, that hurt!). As much as we labor to gain, nothing on this earth will prove profitable or fully satisfying apart from God. As if imitating a woodpecker, we keep pounding our heads upon pursuits. We keep pursuing and never gaining. Our hearts yearn for something that nothing temporal in this life can satisfy. Some have expressed that there is a void or empty place in our heart that cannot be filled with anything but God.

I am not trying to be morbid or ignore the existence of the joy of the Lord. I enjoy my husband, family, ministry, church family and more; however, none of these are designed by God to utterly fulfill me. The joy of the Lord itself is impossible without the Lord who gives the joy. Once I accepted this revelation from God, it changed my expectations of others and personal desires concerning material gain. It helped me to understand myself and internal drives and pursuits. Even when I suffer and experience loss, the fact that eternity is set in my heart reminds me that nothing is permanent upon this earth. Focusing on eternity will help us endure the hard times in this life as well. Abraham knew this (see Heb. 11:8–10).

It is a dangerous thing to pursue anything upon this earth and believe that once you obtain it THEN your life will begin or be fully satisfied. Many a heart has been marooned upon the island of unfulfilling pursuits.

Have you been pursuing something or someone to bring fulfillment to your life? If so, confess this before the Lord and ask Him to come into your life and be your all in all.

Even Solomon with all his wisdom, riches, and achievements, could not find satisfaction upon the earth. Read Ecclesiastes 2:1–11.

We were not created for a temporary existence upon the earth. We were created for eternity—a never-ending fellowship with God. And although Adam and Eve's sin altered things, that eternal yearning and need for fellowship still exists even though we no longer reside in the Garden. Your life is linked to eternity. You were created in the image of God. When your fellowship with God is restored through faith in Jesus Christ, you have the capacity to see beyond the immediate with an eternal perspective. It is really then that Christ sets you in the heavenlies although your physical feet are upon the earth (Eph. 2:4–6).

Still with all of this, we will see in the next lesson that God has not revealed all of life's mysteries to us.

> Indeed before the day was, *I am* He… (Isaiah 43:13 NKJV)

Daily Divine Deliverance

Will you acknowledge and surrender to your eternal call?

Take Time to Say a Personal Prayer of Deliverance.

SESSION 4
WEEK 4: Savoring Your Season

DAY 3: God's Works

I had just given birth and was taken back to my room after recovery. It was a short time before the nurse entered my room and wanted me to stand up and walk. The next thing I remember upon gaining consciousness was my husband carrying me to the bed. I need not fill in all the details, just think of a hospital gown and you'll be very close! I was not happy at all with that nurse. I expected her to know better. But how could she? How could she thoroughly know the wonderful and intricate workings of each human body that came through that door? I am sure she didn't have all the answers about her own physique. Man, with all of his research, has figured out some complexities of the body, but not all. He is in a never-ending pursuit to obtain this knowledge. His hard work has paid off, but is not complete.

* * * * * * * * * * *

You Cannot Find Out God's Works From Beginning To End

In our last lesson, we discussed the pursuits and burden of men to labor hard because of eternity being set in their hearts. Yet man will never find true fulfillment upon the earth apart from God. Having this eternal perspective will permit a person to truly savor their season. However, even this eternal perspective will not allow mankind to know God's works from beginning to end.

Ecclesiastes 3:11 reads:

> *He has made everything beautiful in its time. Also He has put eternity in their hearts,* ***except that no one can find out the work that God does from beginning to end.***

96

Compare the latter part of this verse with Ecclesiastes 8:16–17. What insight can we receive from these verses?

No matter how smart or how much a person labors, they cannot know the sovereign, eternal plan of God in each situation. If they could, they would be omniscient (all knowing) as He is. We see but a part of God's works, not the beginning or its end. Otherwise we would be infinite and not finite. This is the same as a piece of tapestry where we can see all the strokes of the needlework in various colors and shapes on the back, but only God is able to see the finished work completed on the opposite side.

Christ has enlightened us and given us the capacity to understand some eternal things from the revelation of His Word and guidance of His Spirit, but we do not have the same capacity as God to know everything. We need to understand that only God has all the answers to the complex questions of each person's life that appear to be perplexing.

What does Romans 11:33 tell us?

Read Deuteronomy 29:29 and write down what belongs to us and what belongs to God.

Even if we knew the entire Bible from cover to cover with all its Hebrew and Greek meanings, we still would have limited knowledge. Read John 21:25 and write down why this is so.

Call to mind a situation that requires a decision on your part. What info do you have? What info is not clear to you at this time? How can Deuteronomy 29:29 provide comfort to you with some of your unanswered questions?

What did Jesus say to the disciples in Acts 1:7 when asked about the restoration of the kingdom of Israel?

Read Ecclesiastes 3:18–21 to see some assumptions that Solomon made between man and animals.

> Things he knew about man and animals:

 - man and animals have a common mortality – they both die

 - man and animals both come from dust and will return to the dust

 He is not saying that men and animals are the same; rather, He is saying that the dead bodies of men and beasts both putrefy. The difference is the respect that is paid to them by the survivors.

Psalm 49:12 - Nevertheless man, though in honor, does not remain; He is like the beasts that perish.

➢ Things he was uncertain about regarding man and animals include the following:

- Of course, people who are saved through faith in Christ will one day be resurrected to have glorified bodies suitable for the new heavenly home (1 Cor. 15:35 & 40). In verse 21, Solomon's question is directed more toward the spirit of the animal because no one really knows what happens to the spirit of an animal. It is just a rhetorical question because he acknowledges in Ecclesiastes 12:7 that man's spirit goes up to God. Solomon, like all of us, has some knowledge, but not all.

Psalm 49:15 - But God will redeem my soul from the power of the grave, For He shall receive me.

My neighbor died of cancer and had his dog buried with him. I am sure that those who attended his funeral service saw that he and the dog were both lifeless, but could not tell you for sure whether they are together now.

We cannot know God's work from beginning to end, but He is precious enough to reveal some things to us. These are the things that belong to us and our children. We can neither take away nor add anything to our Father's plan.

In closing, please read Ecclesiastes 3:14–15 below.

I know that whatever God does,
It shall be forever.
Nothing can be added to it,
And nothing taken from it.

God does it, that men should
fear before Him.
That which is has already been,
And what is to be has already
been;
And God requires an account
of what is past.

> Why should the Gentiles say, "So where is their God?" But our God is in heaven; He does whatever He pleases. (Psalm 115:2–3 NKJV)

Daily Divine Deliverance

Is there anything you feel you need to inform
God of that He does not know?

Take Time to Say a Personal Prayer of Deliverance.

SESSION 4
WEEK 4: Savoring Your Season

DAY 4: Enjoy What You Labored For

I am in my fifties and realize more each day that life is fleeting. As soon as I wake up, get cleansed and dressed, it's time to wash my face again and get into my nightgown. Seeing the men my sons have grown into and how fast my three grandchildren are growing, causes me to realize the truth of this next passage of Scripture. I have labored in the Word of God most of my life so I may equip and strengthen the Body of Christ and reach the lost who do not know Him. It can become disheartening at times when you see how much emphasis is put on what is seen and what can be measured, even in the church. I have seen some retreat leaders who are more concerned about having money in the budget to pass out printed bags than for the speaker to spread the Word of God, which will live forever. If you think about what I do, there is no true way to measure it. I may plant a seed of the Word that does not germinate for years to come; I may speak at women's functions and never see those women again; I may post something in a newsletter or website and never know the hearts it touches. Although God is gracious in letting me hear testimonies and see fruit in the lives of others, there really is no true way to measure what I do. So God has brought contentment to my soul to enjoy my life and labor, do good continuously, and to rejoice in everything—for this is the gift of God.

* * * * * * * * * * *

Rejoice, Do Good, Enjoy What You Labored For—It Is The Gift Of God

Please read Ecclesiastes 3:12–13 and 22.

Do you: **YES**   **NO**

1. Rejoice daily?   _____   _____
2. Do Good daily?   _____   _____
3. Enjoy what you have labored for?   _____   _____
4. Use each day as a gift from God?   _____   _____

 If not, what seems to hinder you from doing so?

By the grace of God, I purpose to enjoy each day as a gift from God. This is a must if I am to savor the seasons of my life. As much as I love others and have compassion for many, I'm continually learning how not to set my affections on anything down here. I am not talking about being so heavenly minded that I am no earthly good. I believe the principle of eternity being set in my heart by God, and it's Him alone that keeps me in balance between heaven and earth. This is a struggle at times, for the world has many options for trying to replace God in my life. We must be careful not to let anything created replace our Creator!

Here are some other things I do to savor my season:

1. Do not begin a day without first spending time alone with God in His Word and prayer.

2. Learn to respond and not react. Let the Holy Spirit control my emotions and actions so that I do not fly off the handle in my flesh.

3. Flee from pride and boasting. James 1:17 asks a question that keeps me grounded.

4. I know I cannot please everyone. I will go crazy trying to fill the void in someone else's life that only God can fill.

5. Fret for a moment and then get over it. I heard something that stuck with me…

   A *setback* is a *setup* for a *comeback*! I like that!

6. Be careful…for we reap **what** we sow, **more** than we sow, **later** than we sow. Picture a kernel of corn and then a field of corn stalks. Yikes!

7. Remember that all things should be done in love (1 Corinthians, chapter 13)—God's *unconditional* love.

What are some things you can begin to do in obedience to Ecclesiastes 3:12–13 and 22?

What happens to those who determine to eat, drink, and be merry in accordance with their own desires and those of the world? Read Ecclesiastes 11:9.

In Ecclesiastes 5:18–20, the message is the same, but the word *heritage* is used instead of gift. Heritage can be translated as "portion." Chapter 5 makes reference to the man who toils for his possessions versus the rich man who does not. Each has their particular portion from God and should consider it their heritage or gift. Being content with your portion, finding satisfaction and enjoyment in it is a gift from God. Think of the ease with which wealth can slip through one's fingers—we brought nothing into this world at birth and we will take nothing with us when we depart.

Some have taken these verses to mean that you can be a glutton with food and drink all the alcoholic beverages you desire. This is not true. To eat and drink is an expression of companionship. We see in these verses that He wants us to enjoy what we have labored for, but it is the abuse that He condemns. It is when things or others become our idols and life that we grieve God. Jesus did come so we may have life and have it more abundantly! He is not a killjoy! Read Proverbs 10:22.

Let's close our time by making some observations from Ephesians 5:15–21.

There are many ways given whereby we are to redeem our time. List some of them below.

1.

2.

3.

4.

5.

6.

7.

8.

Have you gotten to a place where you can experience enjoyment with your lot? If so, this is a gift from God. I cannot explain it except to say it's freedom of mind and spirit. May our Lord remove any obstacles that are hindering you from enjoying and doing some good with that which you have labored for.

> I cried out to You, O Lord: I said, "You are my refuge, My portion in the land of the living. (Psalm 142:5 NKJV)

Daily Divine Deliverance

Are you content with your portion?

Take Time to Say a Personal Prayer of Deliverance.

SESSION 4
WEEK 4: Savoring Your Season

DAY 5: Savoring is a Choice

This story was shared with me and I thought I would share it with you. There was a blind girl who hated herself just because she was blind. As a matter of fact, she hated everyone except her loving boyfriend. He was always there for her. She said that if she could only see the world, she would marry her boyfriend. One day someone donated a pair of eyes to her and she was able to see everything, including her boyfriend! Her boyfriend asked her, "Now that you can see the world, will you marry me?" The girl was shocked when she saw that her boyfriend was blind too and refused to marry him. Her boyfriend walked away brokenhearted, and later wrote a note to her saying, "Just take care of my eyes, dear."

* * * * * * * * * * *

As we close out this week's session on savoring your season, please realize that you have covered every verse in Chapter 3 of Ecclesiastes. When we began, we said to savor your season you must:

1. Know that God makes everything beautiful in its time (vs. 11, 16–17)

2. He has put eternity in our hearts (vs. 9–11)

3. We cannot find out God's works from beginning to end, so we may revere Him (vs. 11, 18–21 & 14–15)

4. Rejoice, do good, enjoy what we labored for—it is the gift of God (vs. 12–13 & 22)

My prayer is that you will understand these statements and will have a made-up mind to put them into practice so you may enjoy, take pleasure in, and value any season you are experiencing at the present time. In other words, savor your season! Just like the blind girl with her choices; it's your choice. It's up to you.

Solomon was respected for his wisdom and was given honor by many. However, he did not make choices that allowed him to savor the seasons of his life. His wives turned his heart away from God and he ended up using his wisdom to share with us the true meaning of life and that everything the world has to offer is vanity.

We can make foolish or wise decisions. Read the following and note whether the decisions were foolish or wise.

	Foolish	**Wise**
Ecclesiastes 8:11		
Luke 18:28–30		

	Foolish	**Wise**
Luke 12:13–21		
Matt. 6:25–34		

Here are some other ideas to help you savor your season:

1. Walk by faith and not by sight. Have faith in God and not yourself or your abilities.

2. Believe what He says about everything! He is more concerned about building our character and making us like Christ than to load us up with a bunch of material things.

3. As women we defer self to the family, employer, or another. Don't lose sight of who you are. God made you special.

4.	There is something about little children that can bring much joy to any season of your life.

5.	Learn to enjoy your season. Make peace with the aging process—wrinkles, memory lapses, body heading south, and slower pace. There is an old saying, "youth is a gift, but age is a work of art." There is nothing more elegant than a woman looking and acting her age.

6.	One day you will realize you do not have to purchase school supplies, the house is quiet, and trips to the grocery store are fewer. Do not fret over what was or is no longer, but begin to enjoy the present. Do not feed self-pity. For a temporary lift, maybe help another with his or her purchases.

7.	If you are experiencing being a caregiver, needing hormone therapy, experiencing menopause, or having an empty nest, reach out for support. It's not a time to withdraw from others, but the very opposite.

8.	Create a place to resort to and leave the stress behind. Guard a little time each week to recover from the world. If you can, have a time to be pampered and cared for.

9.	Are you experiencing health challenges, loss of power and independence? Is your health taking a toll on your mind, body or spirit? Even in declining health you can continue to enjoy life.

10.	Is someone no longer there for you to talk with? Then ask God to provide an avenue whereby you can meet someone new who will be a source of encouragement in your life.

After reading the above, has the Spirit prompted you with more suggestions?

Looking at Psalm 1, record three wise decisions you can make to savor your season:

1.

2.

3.

To see if you are committing these points to your heart, fill in the blanks below without looking at the other lesson notes:

1. Know that God makes everything

    _____

2. He has put _____ in our hearts

3. We cannot find out God's _____ from
    _____ so we may
    revere Him

4. Rejoice, do good,_____ —
    it is the _____ of God (vs. 12–13, 22)

How did you do? Write these on a card or be creative in keeping these before you until they are a part of your life and you are mindful of them in each season.

Alright, you can begin right now to savor all the seasons of your life. If you purpose to do so in your heart, God will empower you in every way. For of Him and through Him and to Him are all things, to Whom be glory forever! Amen.

> Dead flies putrefy the perfumer's ointment, and cause it to give off a foul odor; so does a little folly to one respected for wisdom and honor. (Ecclesiastes 10:1 NKJV)

Daily Divine Deliverance

What choice will you make today?

Take Time to Say a Personal Prayer of Deliverance.

AFTERWORD

Congratulations! You have been diligent in completing your lessons! I trust your journey with the Lord has been enjoyable. Although your passage through this material has ended, your desire to continually become *"A Woman of All Seasons"* is to be celebrated.

My sister, I have prayed for you ahead of time and for everyone that has reached this point. Please do not forget the material you have learned. It should be a continual part of your life and a steppingstone to future growth. Tell others of this lesson material so they too may grow closer to our Lord.

We know that Jesus Christ is the source of all that pertains to a godly life. The greatest gift one could ever receive is the free gift of salvation provided by faith in Jesus Christ. No matter what your past is, you can experience life anew by following the steps given below. Please realize...

God truly loves you.

"For God so loved the world that He gave His only begotten Son that whosoever believes in Him shall not perish, but have everlasting life." (John 3:16–17 KJV)

But all of us have sinned and separated ourselves from God.

"For all have sinned and fallen short of the glory of God." (Romans 3:23 KJV)

"But your iniquities have separated you from your God, your sins have hidden His face from you so that He will not hear." (Isaiah 59:2 NIV)

Good works, religion, morality, etc. cannot gain your entrance into Heaven with God.

If we decide to do nothing about our sin or if we attempt to be restored with God any other way than through His Son, Jesus Christ, we will be eternally separated from God.

"There is a way that seems right to a man, but the ways thereof are the ways of death." (Proverbs 14:12 KJV)

God has provided the <u>only</u> way to Himself—through His Son, Jesus Christ.

"For there is one God and one mediator between God and men, the man Christ Jesus." (See I Timothy 2:5–6; Acts 4:12)

"But God demonstrates his own love for us in this: While we were still sinners, Christ died for us." (Romans 5:8 NIV)

God loves you so much that He sent His only Son, Jesus, to pay the penalty for **ALL** your sin. Through Jesus' death, burial, and rising to life again, the sins that separated you from God are forgiven and remembered no more.

"...that Christ died for our sins according to the Scriptures, and that He was buried, and that He rose again the third day according to the Scriptures." (1 Corinthians 15:3–4 KJV)

"For Christ also suffered once for sins, the just (Christ) for the unjust (us), that He might bring us to God..." (1 Peter 3:18 KJV)

"...For I will forgive their iniquity, and their sin I will remember no more." (Jeremiah 31:34b NKJV)

You can believe and receive Jesus Christ as your Savior and Lord.

"Yet to all who received Him, to those who believed in His Name, He gave the right to become children of God." (John 1:12 NIV)

"That if you confess with your mouth, 'Jesus is Lord,' and believe in your heart that God raised him from the dead, you will be saved. For it is with your heart that you believe and are justified, and it is with your mouth that you confess and are saved." (Romans 10:9–10 NIV)

"But these are written that you may believe that Jesus is the Christ, the Son of God, and that believing you may have life in His name." (John 20:31 NKJV)

You can receive Him right now by faith through praying:

"Lord Jesus, please forgive me of my sins and come into my life as my Lord and Savior. I believe you paid my sin debt by your death on the cross, being buried, and rising from the grave the third day. I thank you now for your free gift of eternal life, having saved me and forgiven me of all my sins, and placing me into your family. Thank You for coming into my life and empowering me to live for You."

If you prayed this prayer, you are now a child of God—a true Christian!

Your faith in Jesus has given you life eternal! You do not have to be afraid of not going to Heaven or ever being separated from God again! You are on a new journey with Him!

"Everyone who calls on the Name of the Lord will be saved." (Romans 10:13 NIV)

"He who has the Son has life (eternal); he who does not have the Son of God does not have life. I write these things to you who believe in the Name of the Son of God so that you may KNOW that you (now) have eternal life." (I John 5:12–13 NIV)

If you prayed to receive Jesus as your Savior, please email me and let me know. I will send you a Bible if you need one and also a book to help you understand more about your new life and journey as a Christian (a child of God). Praise God! I am so happy about your becoming a part of God's family!

Also, would you be so kind as to contact me about how these lessons have helped you? We would appreciate your comments or suggestions. You can reach me at paula@twmforjesus.org or Transformed Worldwide Ministries, P.O. Box 1071, Exton, PA 19341.

Write me soon! Rejoicing eternally with you—Paula Harris.

ABOUT THE AUTHOR

Paula Harris

Paula resides in Exton, Pennsylvania. She is married and has three sons, a daughter-in-law, and three grandchildren. By the grace of God, Paula has been called and equipped to be a teacher/exhorter. She thanks God for the privilege to travel and share with other women through this teaching ministry. She is a graduate of Lancaster Bible College and Peirce College. She is a certified C.L.A.S.S. Speaker. She is certified by Evangelism Explosion. She has taught Sunday School for more than eighteen years. She is a member of the American Associates of Christian Counselors. Previously, Paula's thoughts of happiness and success were dictated by the world in which she lived, but the Holy Spirit brought about a transformation by the renewing of her mind (Rom. 12:1–2). As a result, her burden is to help other women overcome the world's deception and understand God's perspective on how to live each day. In March of 1985, she began teaching a one-day seminar entitled, "Transformed." Today, she travels and teaches wherever God sends her. One thing is certain: Paula enjoys equipping others in their search for truth from the Word of God. (Please read Zechariah 4:6.)

Paula is the Director of T.W.M. and is **available to speak at your next event**. Call 610-363-2404 or visit www.twmforjesus.org!

"I have known Paula Harris for many years and if I had to give a brief description of her, it would be: Warm, gracious, joyful, loving, courageous, hard working, a student of the Word, and a committed Believer in the Lord Jesus Christ. She stands as a role model for a godly woman in this day and age. Over the past five years, I've been taught and blessed through her teaching ministry, Transformed Worldwide Ministries. Paula has been a keynote speaker for two women conferences hosted by the Montco Bible Fellowship Women's Ministry, of which I am a member. I can confidently say that, on each occasion, Paula delivered Spirit-infused, life application lessons that were thought-provoking, relevant and could only have been possible through fervent prayer and study of the Word. It was also obvious that Paula had painstakingly pondered the best way to present the teachings in order to gain maximum impact, participation, and understanding. By the end of each conference, there was not a dry eye or a life that had not been touched or healed by the Spirit of the Lord." Tyreta Jefferson

REFERENCES

[i]Achtemeier, P. J., Harper & Row, P., & Society of Biblical Literature. (1985). *Harper's Bible dictionary*. Includes index. (1st ed.) (920). San Francisco: Harper & Row.
[ii]Wood, D. R. W., Wood, D. R. W., & Marshall, I. H. (1996, c1982, c1962). *New Bible Dictionary*. Includes index. (electronic ed. of 3rd ed.) (1187). Downers Grove: InterVarsity Press.
[iii]Wuest, K. S. (1997, c1984). *Wuest's word studies from the Greek New Testament : For the English reader* (Eph 5:14). Grand Rapids: Eerdmans.